Different brains Different approaches

1

Huub van Osch

PUBLISHER
BIS Publishers
Building Het Sieraad
Postjesweg 1
1057 DT Amsterdam
The Netherlands
T +31 (0)20 515 02 30
bis@bispublishers.com
www.bispublishers.com

AUTHOR
Huub van Osch MBM
vOSCH The Brand Guide
www.vOSCH.nl
blahblahism
www.blahblahism.com

ISBN 978 90 6369 435 7

Copyright © 2016
Huub van Osch and
BIS Publishers

659.
1
OSC

WORD OF THANKS

Writing a book, in addition to my day job as a creative director, a director of two advertising agencies, a father of two children, and a rich social life, was a real challenge. Still, I'm glad I was able to address this important topic in my field, in an academic context. Writing a book is not only a time-consuming process, but it also offers an escape from everyday life with a very satisfying result as the ultimate goal.

I especially want to thank my professional colleague and right-hand woman Noortje Verbeek for her very dedicated help in designing the book and her unsurpassable commitment to making this book a success. I also want to thank my former colleagues Britt van Mensfoort and Alex Merkx for their significant contribution to the basis of this book.

In particular, I want to thank drs. Marcel van Aalst and PhD Rik Riezebos for their accurate advice during my studies at the Erasmus University in Rotterdam, where I started my research on this challenging topic.

In my immediate circle I want to thank all my friends, acquaintances and colleagues for the many hours they spent reading through the book.

I also want to thank my soulmate and wife Marie-Louise van Osch for her support and all the free hours together we had to miss to make this book a success.

Finally, I want to thank everyone who has in any way been involved or contributed to the development and writing of this book 'Different brains, different approaches' Successful neuro advertising for male and female.

Huub van Osch

TABLE OF CONTENTS

5

PREFACE

In my field, and in my position as creative director, I regularly deal with advertising, which, although intended for both sexes, sometimes resonates better or appeals exclusively to one sex. It becomes a little more complicated to develop tactical or strategic designs as a female creative for a purely masculine brand (and vice versa). Experience shows that strategists and creatives* do not possess sufficient knowledge to effectively communicate the brand to both or individual sexes. One thinks and develops strategies and advertising concepts (without the ability to do otherwise) mainly from the perspective of their own sex. Thus far, little is known about specific knowledge regarding sex differences in communications. The literature on this topic frequently receives little notice, and research on the available literature can lead to grotesque or stereotypical assumptions.

From early childhood, I was raised with the belief that, sociologically speaking, men and women are in fact alike, and that differences were based primarily on culture and education. My mother was a feminist in the early '70s, an ardent supporter of de rode vrouwenbeweging (the red women movement), a group of feminists who contested economic and power imbalances to reduce the social inequality that were rampant at that time. In retrospect, feminism was strongly based on masculine values and in fact sought an unladylike equality. Whatever the case, my mother's fervent commitment to feminist ideals also influenced her private life, which led to my parents' divorce. At the time, it wasn't socially acceptable to assume men and women possibly could think and act differently. This background has confused me for quite a long time, which prevented me from having objective, uninfluenced thoughts.

Effective brand communication is becoming increasingly difficult to achieve, due to a plurality of factors such as fragmentation of the media as a whole and the growing number of media offerings that can successfully claim an individual's limited attention. It is therefore important to increase the effectiveness per communication message. One of the ways to achieve this is through knowledge of the differences in perception and the level of consumer information storage by both sexes. Brands and stakeholders can benefit from this knowledge, creating messages that the complex psyche of the androgynous consumer can more effectively process.

*A recent British study showed that 80% of all purchases worldwide are carried out by women, or are strongly influenced by women. In contrast, 90% of all marketing communications are developed by men (Heijnen, 2004). Gaining more insight into the female super consumer is needed. In addition, large purchases are typically made by men, which makes insight into the male consumer equally important.

GROUP PHOTO HUUB'S MOTHER.
My mother (back row, 2nd from left) was a feminist in the early '70s, an ardent supporter of 'de rode vrouwenbeweging' VOS (Women Orientate themselves in Society), in which economic and power imbalances were contested.

INTRODUCTION . . .

To pragmatically ground the characterisation of male and female in this chapter, I will attempt to explain various dimensions of femininity and masculinity. It is important to keep in mind that the content and theory that will be covered in this book are applicable to Western culture.

I discovered that much laboratory research had been performed on the origin and evolution of sex differences. The theoretical framework (Chapter 2) contains research on animals. It is important to mention that I, personally, when other alternatives are available, am not in favour of animal testing. Some experiments described are from an earlier date and have been useful for science. I also know that this is now being handled in a more nuanced manner.

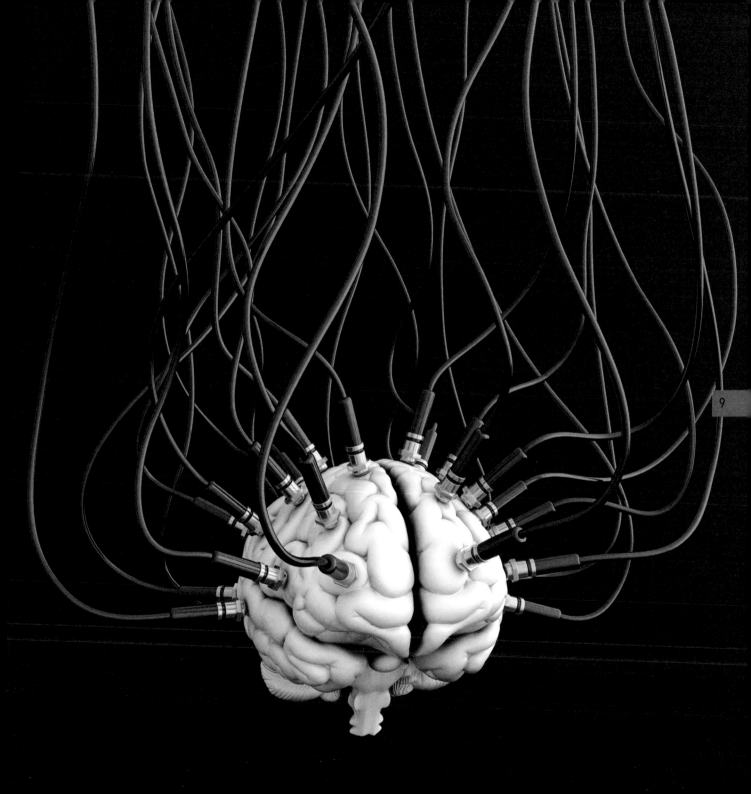

1. THE **ORIGIN** OF **SEX DIFFERENCES**

The differences between men and women can be explained in large part by our biology;

for example, differences with regard to chromosomes, hormones, brain structure and the like,

which will be discussed further in this section. Social and cultural influences are also important.

Structural differences in the brains of men and women will be explained below.

Afterwards, important environmental and evolutionary factors will be discussed.

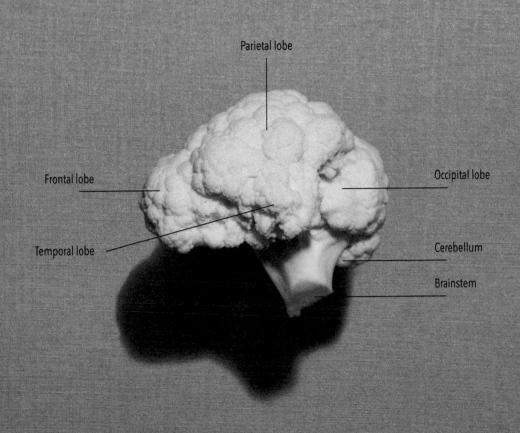

Parietal lobe

Frontal lobe

Occipital lobe

Temporal lobe

Cerebellum

Brainstem

1.1 THE EMBRYONIC PHASE

During fertilisation and the subsequent embryonic development, the foundation is laid for the structure and organisation of the infant's brain. Approximately seven weeks after conception, our unique genes determine whether we will develop into male or female. Each unique gene structure contains 46 chromosomes: 23 from the father and 23 from the mother. Twenty-two of each chromosome are fused with each other and form pairs of chromosomes, which are decisive for physical characteristics such as the colour of the hair and the eyes, the length of the body, the shape of the nose, eyes and ears, et cetera. The last pair of chromosomes determines the sex. Fertilisation with two X chromosomes (the mother always provides an X chromosome) will usually lead to a girl. Fertilisation with an X and a Y chromosome will usually lead to a boy (Malfroot, Brugada, Maselis, Van Damme and Van Middelem, 2013). Eventual development of the embryo into a male or a female depends on the availability or deprivation of the male or female hormone. Disruptions in the supply of the male hormone ultimately determine whether an individual will function entirely masculine or feminine. In other words, an embryo with the latent qualities of the male sex will, with an insufficient supply of testosterone, eventually physically develop into a girl. Many studies have been performed on this subject; Chapter 1 of this book will elaborate on some of them. The studies were conducted on people with hereditary diseases and by carrying out animal tests on rhesus monkeys and rats. The studies show that the amount of both the male and female hormones is the decisive, sex-determining factor (Sterling, 2000; Moir and Jessel, 1991).

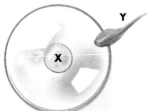   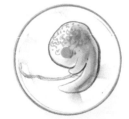 

PHASE 1
Before fertilisation takes place, the Y-chromosome is decisive for the male sex.

PHASE 2
The fertilisation by a Y-chromosome and an X-chromosome takes place, and cell division is initiated.

PHASE 3
The female foetus starts to develop testosterone, which is important for the physical male sex.

PHASE 4
If the testosterone supply falters this will impact the physical male sex.

PHASE 5
When the testosterone supply is not disturbed, the embryo will physically develop all male properties.

1.2 NEUROLOGICAL WIRING AND STRUCTURE

If the embryo is latently feminine, little will change in the basic structure of the brain; thus, we could conclude that the basic structure of the brain is feminine. Things are different in male embryos, given the intervention of testosterone is crucial for morphing the brains of naturally female embryos into males.

The male embryo experiences a surge of testosterone from his developing testes about 7 weeks after conception with the Y chromosome, making the physical male characteristics visible. The testosterone level is four times higher at this time than in the early childhood and teenage years. This increase in testosterone level is repeated during the transition to adolescence when sexuality will develop. With development of the physical male sex in the foetus, testosterone begins to form the structure of the brain into a male pattern. However, when the genitals produce insufficient testosterone, the brain will not fully develop as male, and in the most extreme case the brain remains female. This situation will eventually lead to a boy being born with a female brain. Conversely, it is also possible that after the physical development of the female sex, the embryo receives too large a dose of testosterone from its mother; thus, the female brain might remain partially or entirely undeveloped. Once the brain ultimately evolves to either male or female, it can no longer be affected by hormones (Moir & Jessel, 1991).

PHASE 6
The testes of the child must now ensure the flow of testosterone to the brain.

PHASE 7
All embryonic brains are female in origin, but those with a Y-chromosome are modified in stages to form the male brain structure.

PHASE 8
During this process the corpus callosum narrows, which allows for the transfer of information between the left and right brain.

PHASE 9
The brain specialisations are now developing. If insufficient testosterone is supplied, portions of the brain will remain female.

PHASE 10
The origin of the gender-role centre. This phase occurs only in puberty and creates typical male behaviour; e.g., aggressiveness.

Much research has established a link between the sex hormone testosterone and an increase in aggression. The testosterone level in young men is higher, on average, which probably increases aggression. Testosterone is also associated with increased independence, an urge to compete, assertiveness and self-confidence. Although both sexes create the hormone testosterone (at lower levels in women), the structure of the male brain is more easily influenced by this hormone.

In the following, a number of studies will be reviewed concerning the matters discussed above. Studies have been performed on people with hereditary diseases and on rhesus monkeys and rats. These studies have shown that both male and female hormones are decisive factors in determining gender (Sterling, 2000).

Around the 1950s and 1960s, male or female hormones were regularly administered to treat pregnancy complications. Pregnant women with diabetes were at higher risk of spontaneous miscarriage, caused by one of the adverse effects of diabetes: a shortage of the female hormone oestrogen in the blood. A common treatment at that time to prevent miscarriage was diethylstilbestrol (DES), a synthetic female hormone. It was later discovered that, if the child had been a male embryo, DES had irreversibly changed the development of his brain, and thus the behaviour of the boy at a later age.

Sixteen years later, the boys who had been exposed to DES in the womb were investigated; it was found that the boys in the studied group were distinctly timid and insecure and had low self-esteem. They were also significantly worse at sports than other boys of the same age who had not been exposed to DES and were frequently bullied because they did not have the same dominance and focus on status as the 'regular guys'. The boys in the studied group also had little or no interest in engineering, mathematics or chemistry; things that did interest the members of the investigated group of brothers who had not been exposed to DES. Exposure to hormone treatment with DES in this group of boys had, in the critical phase, prevented development of their brains into the male structure. Conversely, women who suffered from toxaemia (preeclampsia) were treated with the male hormone testosterone. In later life, the daughters of these mothers had little or no interest in clothes, dolls or children and achieved better than average results in science subjects than their female peers (Reinisch & Saunders, 1984).

Diethylstilbestrol (DES, stilboestrol)

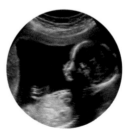

Foetus infected with DES

Regularly monitoring the foetus

1.3 RESEARCH ON ANIMAL EXPERIMENTS

Much research has been performed on rats with regard to the developing brain. The rat brain develops a male or female structure only after birth. The male rat is born with a brain comparable to the brain development of a 7-week-old embryo. After castration, the brain of the male rat develops into a female brain. This outcome is manifested by licking less aggressively and demonstrating submissive and caring behaviour. However, the longer the delay in castration, the less feminine the castrated rat will behave. The male rat brain appears to exploit the lengthened exposure to testosterone to assemble male structures and circuits. As soon as the rat brain has completely developed, it is no longer possible to give the castrated rat his male identity back under the influence of male hormones. An adult castrated rat treated with female hormones exhibits the sexual behaviour of a female rat and curves his spine in the presence of male rats; a sign of subservience. In addition to some minor differences, the castrated rat has the brain of a female in the body of a male rat. This experiment also works the other way. If a newborn female rat is treated with a high dose of male hormones it will mentally develop as a male. It will show more aggression and will attempt to mount other females. Administration of the male or female hormone in the critical phase can therefore provide structural changes to the brain (Moir & Jessel, 1991).

Similar experiments were conducted on songbirds and rhesus monkeys. Some songbird types, in which only the male sings, were treated with the male hormone testosterone; the initially female brains were influenced so that these birds were also able to sing (Moir & Jessel, 1991).

Animal experiments with rhesus monkeys show that testosterone treatment during various stages of pregnancy can evoke male-specific behaviours in female offspring. Young rhesus monkeys were much noisier and, with maternal treatment with testosterone at a later stage, the offspring were more aggressive than their peers (Moir & Jessel, 1991).

The rat is a popular laboratory animal

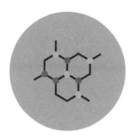

Testosterone hormone

1.4 DISCUSSION

The creation of male and female brains, and their associated behaviour in humans and animals, is not something that is accomplished in a short time, but a process that develops in stages. In each critical stage, neural circuits are formed and destroyed under the influence of hormones to ultimately form a male or female structure (McEwen, 1992). The masculinity or femininity of the brain is perfected in puberty. During this period, the amount of male or female hormone increases to its highest point and the previously rudimentary properties are strengthened. In boys at puberty, testosterone levels suddenly increase to a level no less than 20 times higher than the female hormone (Severson, 2013). As is reflected in the studies described above, hormones are therefore crucial in the formation of the male or female structure.

The amount of the hormones present determines the degree of femininity or masculinity of the individual in question, which also means that gender cannot be considered as a duality, but rather as a continuum with masculine on one side and feminine on the other, and each individual is located somewhere along this scale. Of course, there are also exceptions to this scale, in the form of syndromes, which will be discussed briefly below.

Further research by observation of the brain structures brought other gender differences to light.
The neocortex in the right brain of male rats appears to be considerably thicker. In female rats this was the opposite. Thus, we can conclude that significant similarities can be observed between the male and female brains of rodents, birds, primates and humans. There are many other human behaviours that resemble those of animals. It's not just young male rats that play aggressively or young female monkeys who like to hold a baby and cuddle. Conversely, it's not just men who can read maps better. Nevertheless, male rats are better at finding an exit in a system of corridors than female rats (Moir & Jessel, 1991).

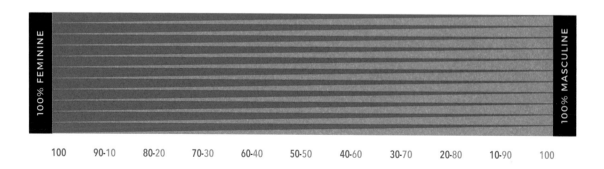

100% FEMININE — 100% MASCULINE

| 100 | 90-10 | 80-20 | 70-30 | 60-40 | 50-50 | 40-60 | 30-70 | 20-80 | 10-90 | 100 |

1.5 SYNDROMES

Various syndromes can occur due to the malfunction of hormones involved in the formation of sex and related gender behaviour. In congenital adrenal hyperplasia (CAH), there is a disturbance in the production of enzymes involved in the formation of sex hormones. In children with XX chromosomes this can lead to the development of male physical characteristics at birth or later, such as a deep voice and a masculine hair pattern.
With androgen insensitivity syndrome (AIS), the receptors for testosterone in the cell wall are no longer functioning; thus, testosterone is not recognised and is not registered. As a result, children with the XY chromosome are born with highly feminised sex organs and they develop breasts and a female form during puberty.

KLINEFELTER SYNDROME
Klinefelter syndrome is the most common syndrome related to sex chromosomes in males. Men with this syndrome have an extra X chromosome (XXY) and produce less and less testosterone during puberty. These men develop more feminine forms and less muscle. They also appear to have lower self-esteem and a more moody, unstable state of mind (Sterling, 2000).

TURNER SYNDROME
Extremely feminine behaviour is observed in women with Turner syndrome. These women are missing the X chromosome, which is why they have an 'XO' as genetic code. Women with the Turner syndrome do not have ovaries. The ovaries of normal women produce small amounts of testosterone, which exerts some influence on the development of the female brain. Women with Turner syndrome do not experience this influence; therefore, their brains will develop an extremely feminine structure. Turner syndrome usually has little impact on mental faculties; however, their aptitude for science, spatial awareness and sense of direction were found to be well below average. Furthermore, their behaviour is extremely feminine; for example, they play only with dolls, dream about babies, are extremely romantic and devote exceptionally much attention to their grooming (Moir & Jessel, 1991).

2. HOW 500 MILLION YEARS OF EVOLUTION HAS AFFECTED BOTH SEXES

The modern human we experience now is the result of an adjustment process lasting

millions of years, during which the brain has evolved in stages. These phases still form the

base of our current brain. This chapter provides insight into how the brain has developed

during this evolution, influence by a different division of tasks in a prehistoric community

that effects modern society.

This is our mutial ancestor,
uncle Babatunde, from
a prehistoric tribe in Ethiopia,
about 160 000 year ago.

2.1 SPECIALISATION

In prehistoric times, there was already a division of labour between the sexes, which eventually led to a degree of physical specialisation. We can also suppose that at the same time there was a certain degree of mental specialisation. In prehistoric times, the primary tasks of men were hunting, defence and protection of the tribe, reproduction and building settlements. For example, men had to become proficient in creating, maintaining and repairing weapons, cabins and tools. Women are mainly portrayed as collectors of (among other things) plants, bearers of children and organisers of social life (Frankplads, 2013; Waguespack, 2005).

2.2 LOAD BALANCING

Hunting requires a substantial demand for visual and spatial abilities to orient yourself in a field and to be able to accurately hit prey. The focus is on long-term persistent pursuit and concentrating on long-term goals. A group of men had to be able to perform on a team and be capable of dealing with one sole problem, ignoring distracting side issues. Sometimes, to catch large prey, men were away from home for an extended period of time and to not be noticed, spoke as little as possible. For men, it was better to have less empathy; otherwise, in terms of killing prey, they might begin to doubt attacking a herd to which adults and young animals belong. Men were more expendable than women in terms of preproduction; therefore, risky actions had to be performed by men.

The primary tasks of women were as follows: safety for herself and her children; communication within the community; social skills; successful reproduction; and fine locomotion to learn hand skills, such as making footwear, baskets and fishing nets, and learning techniques such as braiding, crocheting and weaving. To hold a community together it was imperative that small conflicts were quickly resolved before they grew larger. For this, social and communication skills were necessary (Frankplads, 2013). In a social community with many members of different age groups, a certain chaos theory is in force, in which it is (sometimes) required to execute multiple tasks simultaneously and to distribute concentration over several areas (Murphy, 1996). Also, the fear and disgust of spiders, snakes and other insects is important for the safety of defenceless children and babies. During puberty, for example, the aversion to insects grows twice as strong in women as in men. Research has shown that just before adolescence, the love of girls for domestic animals such as horses and rabbits are three-fold greater than in boys of the same age (Frankplads, 2013; Hansen, 2002).

2.3 EVOLUTION OF PSYCHOLOGY

Women traditionally ranged over a much smaller territory. Since prehistoric times, their world has been located closer to their place of residence. One consequence is that they pay more attention to issues that require attention in the immediate vicinity (Key, 2005).

Also, women notice and compare themselves to each other to a much higher degree. Women will ask themselves: 'How will I do this and how should I approach her in this situation?' Not all women are equally fanatic about this. Sometimes more, and sometimes less. This pugnacity perhaps stems from evolutionary psychology, where women were forced to survive in a community and they wanted to avoid being dominated by another woman (Wolff, 2005).

In contrast, men can better distinguish the substance from the side issues. This can be good in one situation and not necessarily in another. This probably has something to do with evolutionary psychology, and especially hunting. During the hunt men had to be able to concentrate on one thing. Men were responsible for certain foods such as meat. Women remained behind to take care of the children (De Jong, 2005).

2.4 PHYSICAL AND MENTAL DIFFERENCES

Men were responsible for the physically heavier duties and for the defence of a living community. They were also physically better equipped for this. The adult body of a man is on average 30% stronger, and men have almost twice as much muscle mass as women. The hand of a woman has on average two-thirds of the power of a man. Men also have larger jaws and a bigger nose than women (Frank Pads, 2013). Overall, men have an athletic body that is equipped to deliver physical performance, and can therefore handle dangerous situations better while hunting. In addition, they are mentally independent, assertive, dominant and more self-centred. On the other hand, they have less empathy than women.

Women were physically less strong and were dominated more often, so they developed a submissive role. The superior empathy of a woman probably originated there. Subordinate people are often exceptionally good at interpreting the facial expressions of their superiors. The excellent ability of women to read emotions might partly come from the fact that women for a very long time have been regarded as the inferior sex. This empathic ability, however, is very welcome for the care of infants, young children, the elderly and pets because these are less able to explain themselves and they may suffer temporary imbalances. Medically speaking, women are stronger. They suffer less from illnesses and are less often a victim of accidents. Also, at birth there is a lower risk of death and deformity (Frankplads, 2013).

2.5 DIFFERENCES IN NEUROBIOLOGY

As mentioned in the previous chapter, our present brain is the result of 500 million years of evolution (Franzen, 2004). The brain can be viewed as a three-part unit, which is based on the brain's origin and evolution (MacLean, 1973). These three parts are the protoreptilian brain, the limbic system and the neocortex. These represent the evolution phases: reptile-mammal-human. These systems (though not precisely defined) differ in age, pursue different interests, obey different laws and might not work optimally with each other. We can roughly characterise them as instinct, emotion and intellect (Vroon, 2006).

THE PROTOREPTILIAN BRAIN

The protoreptilian brain, which originated 500 million years ago, consists of the brainstem and the spinal cord (Franzen, 2004). This part of the brain controls primary physiological needs, such as drinking, eating, watching, blood pressure, body temperature and the discharge and regulation of muscle tension. Its primary function is to achieve and maintain a status-quo; it controls the body's autonomic processes (Franzen & Bouwman, 1999).

THE LIMBIC SYSTEM

The limbic system, or paleocortex (which originated 200 million years ago), was described by MacLean in 1954 and includes a part of the forebrain, the limbic system itself and the cingulate cortex (is seen as a precursor to the neocortex). This system is primarily responsible for emotions; emotional memory, short-term memory and the expressive reactions that are important for our self-preservation, such as joy, anger, fear, sadness, excitement and boredom. We have this part of the brain in common with other mammals. In humans, it is responsible for ingrained motivations, such as women's caring and to social nature, and men's desire to protect, organise, fight and prevail. The limbic system is very sensitive to analogue communication, such as observations based on posture, facial expressions, scent and sound (Franzen & Bouwman, 1999).

THE NEOCORTEX

The neocortex, or cerebral cortex, originated 50,000 years ago and contains approximately 20% of all our neurons (brain cells). It is composed of the left and the right cerebral hemisphere. The neocortex is the centrepiece of the so-called higher brain functions, such as language, mathematics, analysis, music, ethics, morals and other specifically human characteristics (Franzen & Bouwman, 1999).

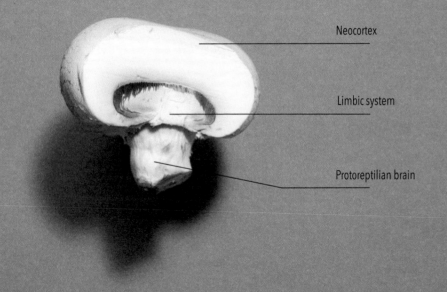

Neocortex

Limbic system

Protoreptilian brain

3. WIRING, ORGANISATION AND NEURAL CIRCUITS OF THE SEXES

Discover the neurobiology of the brain and the significant differences in the structure of

both sexes. The male and female brain seems to be organised differently, pursue different

goals, and work under the influence of other hormones which is why both genders perceive

the world differently. This often causes small conflicts in daily life, but in the end, they

complement each other perfectly.

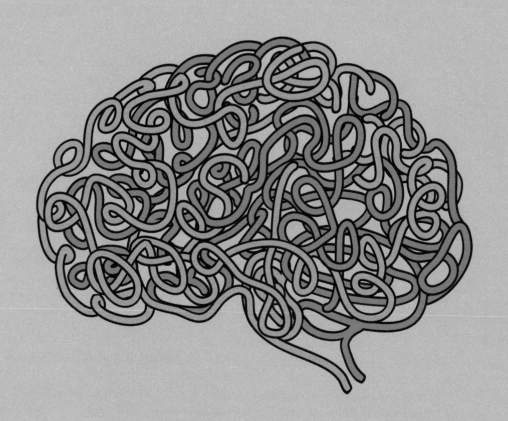

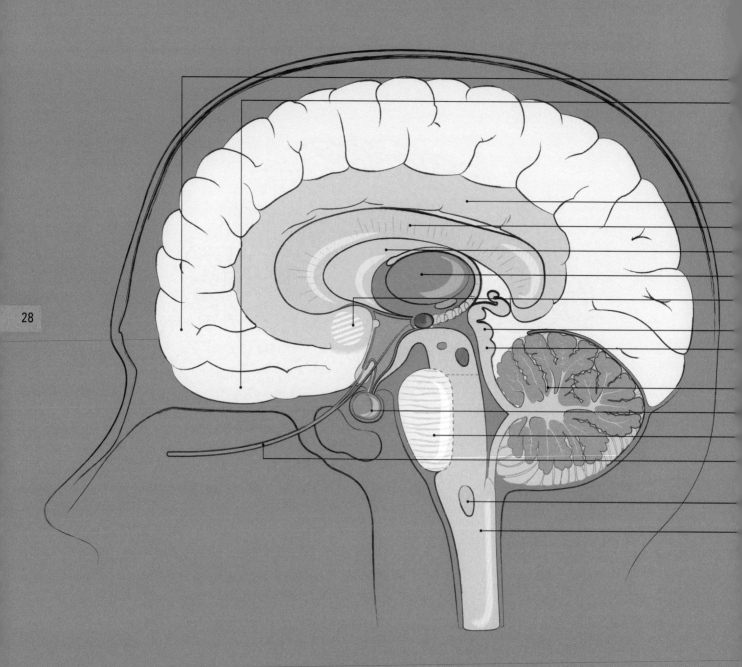

28

3.1 ANATOMY OF THE BRAIN

Prefrontal cortex (PFC)

Ventromedial prefrontal cortex (vmPFC)

Cingulate cortex (CG)

Corpus callosum (CC)

Septum pellucidum (SP)

Thalamus (THALM)

Nucleus accumbens (NA)

Superior colliculus

Inferior colliculus

Cerebellum

Pituitary gland (PIT)

Pons

Olfactory bulb (OB)

Medulla (MED)

Brainstem (BS)

Pineal gland (PI)

Habenular commissure

Posterior commissure

Tectum (corpora quadrigemina)

Red nucleus

Substantia nigra (SN)

Pons

Fourth ventricle

Insular cortex/insula (INS)

Fornix

Mammillary body

Thalamus (THALM)

Hippocampus (Hip)

Subthalamus

Amygdala (AMY)

Superior colliculus

Anterior commissure

Hypothalamus (H)

Ventral tegmental area (VTA)

Optic chiasma

Pituitary gland (PIT)

Olfactory bulb (OB)

3.2 SPECIALISATION IN THE LEFT AND RIGHT CEREBRAL HEMISPHERE

The variations in the predisposed brain structure as described in Chapter 2.1 are completed during puberty. Male and female hormones rise to their peak level during this period, strengthening the existing rudimentary gender properties. Puberty starts fairly suddenly for boys, with testosterone levels rising to a level no less than 20x higher than the female hormone (Severson, 2013). In women, the left cerebral hemisphere is slightly thicker than in men, which indicates a more developed left cerebral hemisphere. This is also where the linguistic part of the brain is located. On average, women perform better when carrying out linguistic tasks such as grammar, spelling, oral expression, writing and reading. In women, the linguistic area is located in just one place: the foremost part of the left cerebral hemisphere, which makes that area better equipped for

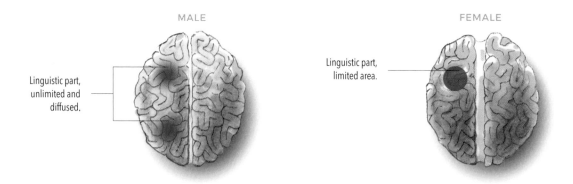

MALE

FEMALE

Linguistic part,
unlimited and
diffused.

Linguistic part,
limited area.

specialisation. This is why girls tend to learn to speak earlier than boys; this part of the brain is more efficiently organised for speech. In men, the linguistic area is located in both the foremost part, as well as the rearmost part of the left cerebral hemisphere; this type of organisation is less effective (Moir & Jessel, 1991).

3.3 COMMUNICATION BETWEEN THE LEFT AND RIGHT CEREBRAL HEMISPHERE

According to research, the corpus callosum or callosal commissure, which enables the exchange of information between the left and right cerebral hemisphere, appears to be approximately 12% thicker and more rounded in women than in men (Rozendaal, 2002). This corpus callosum provides a larger number of neural interconnections in women than in men, which improves information transfer between the cerebral hemispheres. In other words, women use both cerebral hemispheres during their thinking process, allowing them to reach a more balanced judgement on issues. In return, fewer specialisations take place when compared with men. Men have shown less cooperation between the left and right cerebral hemisphere, which makes them less effective in associating cognition and affection.

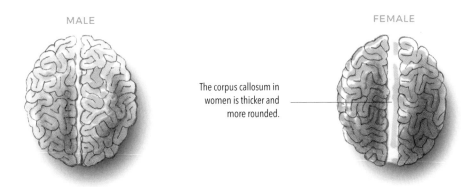

MALE

FEMALE

The corpus callosum in women is thicker and more rounded.

This has the disadvantage of men drawing less balanced conclusions than women in a combined affective and cognitive problem. On the other hand, a man is able to come to a conclusion more quickly because he is not hampered by a cognitive or affective value judgement. He simply is not able to have both cerebral hemispheres work well together The more 'specialised and limited' neurological processes in a man ensure that he can reach a height of genius in one concentrated area after adolescence (Kimura, 1992).
The specialised male brain experiences less distraction when concentrating; however, there is a lot more that can go wrong. It is often said that genius is close to madness, and there is an element of truth in that.

3.4 EFFECTS OF HORMONAL INFLUENCES

According to research published by the Statistics Netherlands/Centraal Bureau voor Statistiek, based on the results of primary and secondary education, girls are ahead of boys when it comes to educational performance. They finish university faster and do not drop out as often. Women have an easier time achieving excellence in education than men. They are more accurate, more serious and choose their education based on intrinsic motivation. Later in life, men overtake women in most areas. In particular, they excel in areas that are a consequence of the male exploratory and technical character. Specific knowledge due to their focus (testosterone) and their higher self confidences (testosterone) makes it easier to excel in certain areas. Of all Dutch professors only 14.8% are women, and in large Dutch companies the proportion of female managers remains at 20% (Gerritsen, Verdonk & Fisher, 2012; Koolen, 2014). There are several influences, however, such as the expectation of the traditional female role and the limited opportunities given to women from (male) superiors.

Considerable research has established a link between testosterone and an increase in aggression. The testosterone level in young males is higher than in older men, on average, which presumably increases aggression as well. Testosterone is also associated with an increase in independence, the urge to compete, self-assertion and self-confidence.

Although both sexes create testosterone (at a low level in women), the structural construction of the male brain is more influenced by this hormone. One might conclude that women generally have a more considered thought process without the influence of this hormone. It should be noted, however, that communication between the two cerebral hemispheres sometimes causes more confusion, impeding effective reasoning. A woman might be less able to separate feelings and intellect from one another (Moir & Jessel, 1991).

From the study of animals, we know that they have a seasonal reproductive function. The production of sex hormones fluctuates over time. But what about humans? Men produce the most testosterone at the end of the fall and in early winter; they produce the least in the spring (Dabbs & Dabbs, 2001). In women, we see monthly fluctuations in progesterone and oestrogen according to the menstrual cycle.

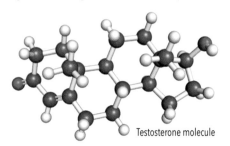
Testosterone molecule

32

3.5 CONCLUSION

One might conclude that women generally have a more considered thought process. Women use a cognitive and affective consideration process when making a decision, which causes them to need more time when making a choice. It should be noted that communication between the two hemispheres can sometimes cause confusion, which constitutes an impediment to effective reason. A woman is likely less capable of separating feelings and rationality from each other (Moir & Jessel, 1991). The female decision process is also affected by a lower sense of self-confidence, which is why women are more likely to choose small or several small purchases.

Men are less or not at all able to make a balanced assessment and they base their purchases purely on a rational or emotional decision. An emotional decision is made based on the urge to compete and a greater self-confidence; thus, men tend to overestimate themselves and, as a result, they make less frequent but larger purchases.

4. SENSORY DIFFERENCES

Nearly all communication with which we are confronted every day enters through

our senses. These senses are directly connected to the brain and particularly with our

emotion. Cognition analyses it, but emotion gets us to move. The senses of men

and women sometimes are controlled by different parts of the brain, are built differently

in some aspects and are sometimes sharper.

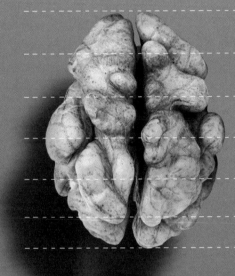

Higher mental functions

Eye movement and orientation

Initiation of voluntary muscles

Sensory

Somatosensory association

Vision

MALE

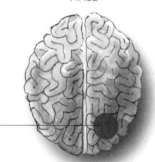

Spatial and visual
skills are sharply limited
in men, and are therefore
more efficiently
organised.

36

FEMALE

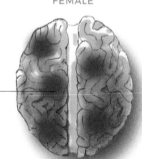

Spatial and visual
skills in women are
diffuse, and are therefore
less efficiently
organised.

4.1 SPATIAL AND VISUAL ABILITIES

Visual perception is a very complex system in the brain, about which much is now known. It is also, for both men and women, one of the fastest acting senses. Notable differences between the sexes can be recognised here. 'Spatial and visual skills' (visuospatial perception) are better in men than in women. In men, these skills are more sharply limited in the right brain hemisphere and are organised more efficiently. In the processing of abstract problems, men use only the right brain hemisphere.

The superiority of men's visuospatial perception was evident in experiments in which the electrical activity of boys' and girls' brains was measured during a spatial assignment. They had to find a way to fold an unfolded piece of paper into a three-dimensional shape. In the boys, this process proved to run more efficiently, and the right cerebral hemisphere was constantly active; whereas, with the girls, electrical activity was shown in both brain hemispheres (Moir & Jessel, 1991).

Men are better map-readers and are better able to mentally rotate or manipulate three-dimensional objects. Their spatial cognitive ability is also better developed, resulting in a better sense of direction and greater insight into spatial relationships. A man uses more verbal expressions, such as left and right, when describing an itinerary, whereas women make more use of landmarks, such as 'make a left turn after passing the red tower'. It is also known that women more often confuse the terms left and right.

Look at the first shape and assign a shape that is not equal.

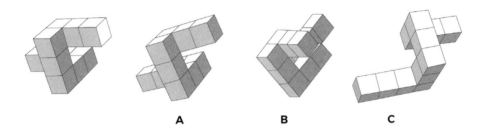

A **B** **C**

With their spatial awareness and aptitude for three-dimensional thinking, this is an example of a test that should not be difficult for men.
(The correct answer is b)

In women, visual stimuli are observed by both the left and right brain hemispheres. This observation indicates a less specialised location in the brain, making it work less efficiently. However, when a woman is treated with the male hormone testosterone, the results directly improve when performing spatial assignments. The action of testosterone in females is less effective than in men because the structure of the female brain is less sensitive to this hormone (Kimura, 1992).

On the other hand, high hormone levels have a positive effect on coordination. At a young age, girls are superior in tasks that demand fast, precise and delicate movements such as knitting, embroidery or crafting with paper. This shows that the cerebellum, where the motor skills are seated, has a more refined organisation in women. Visually, significant differences are also observable. Men and women, because of their different neural wiring, perceive the world differently. A female baby reacts, at this early stage of development, earlier to people than to things. For male babies however, there is no difference in reaction to a coloured ball or a human being. The boy will exhibit an almost equal emotion from both stimuli. Women have a significantly developed empathy at an early age so that they can better recognise primary emotions or mood nuances on the human face, such as sadness, joy or disgust.

Intriguing research results show that men are not inclined to see the visual field in a wide angle. Their field of view is more narrow than women's, and can be described as a kind of tunnel vision. On the other hand, men have a sharper view at long distances.

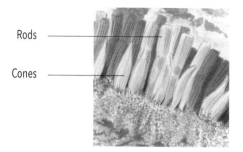

Rods

Cones

This figure clearly shows where the cones are located in the eye. The cones are responsible for the observation of three colours: red, green and blue. The rods provide the perception of black and white and shades of grey.

38

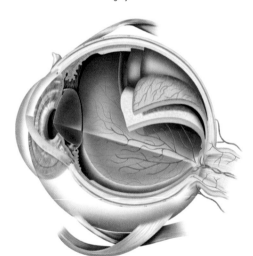

This figure shows how the entering light is split through the lens onto the retina in various wavelengths and is converted into electrical impulses. These impulses (stimuli) are then transported to the visual cortex via the thalamus. The visual cortex translates these data into a visual perception.

Women have a wider field of view because they have more light-sensitive rods and cones in their retinas, leading the eye to capture more light pulses from a wider area. Thus, a woman also needs less light and they can see better in the dark. By contrast, men see better in bright light than women. Because their retina possesses more cones, women generally see more colours and perceive them as more intense. This enhanced perception is possible because the visual perception in women is divided between the left and right cerebral hemisphere so that both the cognitive and affective stimuli can reinforce each other through the corpus callosum.

The corpus callosum is thicker and more convex in women and has a larger number of connections, increasing the transfer of information between the two brain hemispheres. In addition, the left cerebral hemisphere in women (where, in contrast to males, emotions are also represented) is larger than the right cerebral hemisphere. This is reversed in men. Women tend to prefer blue above red, whereas men prefer red. Women are also more sensitive to light from the low-frequency part of the spectrum and can see more shades of blue than men; their visual memory is also better developed (Moir & Jessel, 1991).

Approximately 1 in 12 men (about 8%) has a colour perception disorder, also known as anomalous trichromats. The most common anomalous trichromat is the disorder in perceiving the colours red (protanomaly) and green (deuteranomaly). This colour disturbance is passed on to men through the X-chromosome. Men, in contrast to women, have only one X chromosome, thus errors in this chromosome show abnormalities more often than in women. This X-chromosome contains the genes for the red- and green-sensitive cones, whereas the blue-sensitive cones are located on an entirely different chromosome. That explains why anomalous trichromacy has a genetic cause and almost exclusively appears in men. It may also happen that one or more colours cannot be observed.

This is called dichromasy, a defect in which the colour red (protanopia) and/or green (deuteranopia) cannot be detected. Complete colour blindness (monochromacy), with no cones present on the retina, rarely occurs (Brettel, Vienot & Mollon, 2004). Dichromacy occurs by deviation only in 1 in 200 (0.5%) women. People who see colours normally are called trichromats.

Anomalous trichromat			men	women
1	Protanomaly	red malfunction	1 %	0,02 %
2	Deuteranomaly	green malfunction	4,9 %	0,38 %
3	Tritanomaly	blue malfunction	0,001 %	0,001 %
Dichromats				
4	Protanopia	red defect	1,1 %	0,01 %
5	Deuteranopia	green defect	1,5 %	0,002 %
6	Tritanopia	blue defect	0,0025 %	0,0025 %

Anomalous trichromat diagram: This diagram shows how often anomalous trichromat and dichromat abnormalities occur in men, and to a lesser extent in women.

An extremely rare superior colour perception that occurs only in women is called tetrachromacy. These are women who can perceive four colour channels instead of three. This can occur due to chromosomal errors that relate to the perception of colour, which could cause the following remarkable result. On one of the X-chromosomes the red or green pigment genes can vary lightly from each other while the other X-chromosome carries normal pigment genes. Due to the biological phenomenon of the X-inactivation, making some cells focus on the one X-chromosome and the remaining cells on the other, this can lead to a female eye with four different cones: blue, green, red and a light variety of red. Although a successful test has been developed for this scientific theory, it should be noted that testing is difficult because so few tetra chromatic women are available for such tests. Still, I think this research is worth mentioning here because it appears that only women can develop as tetrachromats, allowing women, genetically significant, to possess more genes for perceiving colour (De Vaal, 2000).

Deuteranopia (green defect)

Protanopia (red defect)

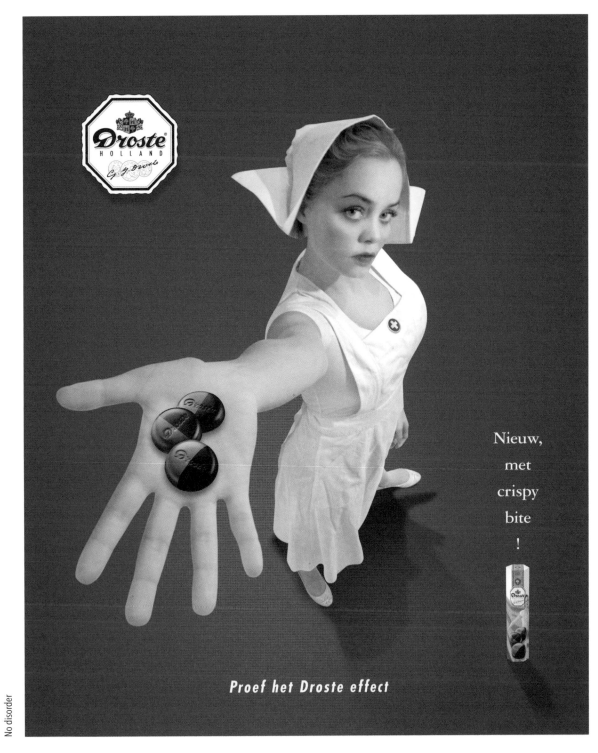

Nieuw,
met
crispy
bite
!

Proef het Droste effect

AGENCY: vOSCH THE BRAND GUIDE, OISTERWIJK
'New, with crispy bite! Taste the Droste effect'

4.2 THE OLFACTORY SYSTEM

Women generally have a more sensitive sense of smell than men. They easily recognise a scent and find it easier to grant a linguistic meaning to it. Women can be up to 110x more sensitive to some fragrances. Ovulating women are able to detect the state of a man's immune system from his perspiration. Based on reproduction, they prefer men with a different immune system than themselves so that their children's DNA is better equipped (Rozendaal, 2002). In addition, women can perceive exaltolide well, a synthetic musk-like odour that belongs to the natural scent palette of men, whereas men are almost insensitive to this scent (Moir & Jessel, 1991). This theory confirms a similar experience I had as a spectator at an event in which blindfolded women had to find their partner by smell only. This turned out to not be a problem in many cases. The reverse was proven for men, for whom in all cases finding their partner by smell was considerably more difficult. The olfactory system is a remarkable sense because it follows a different pathway in the brain than the other senses. Fragrance is the most abstract perception and is difficult to define; probably because smell (olfactory bulb), in contrast to almost all other sensory information, does not pass through the thalamus, where the stimulus is interpreted and passed on to a specialised section in the neocortex. Smell stimuli, however, pass through amygdala (AMY) and the hippocampus (short term memory) and, above all, smell stimuli call on episodic connections from the episodic memory, the collection of the memories of numerous events

(Potts, 1994). Fragrances are suggestive, stimulate associations and evoke emotions (Schaffelaar, 1999). At the end of the hippocampus one finds the almond core, or amygdala. All the information that comes in through our various senses passes through the amygdala. There is a hypothesis that the amygdala acts as a storehouse of emotions (emotional memory) like the one for odours. Women have a significantly broader emotional spectrum, and are more likely to achieve a higher response from the stimuli of the olfactory system.

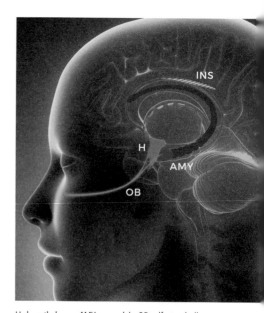

H - hypothalamus, AMY - amygdala, OB - olfactory bulb, INS - insular cortex (insula)
Smell is highly developed in women. The epithelium on the palate contains between six and ten million olfactory cells that send impulses to the brain.

4.3 THE GUSTATORY SPECTRUM

There are strong indications that the taste buds
of both sexes also differ. Women tend to be more
susceptible to quinine (bitter taste) and have
a preference for sweet foods. Men, on the other
hand, can better distinguish salty flavours.
Generally, studies indicate that women have a more
sensitive gustatory sense. It is worth noting that the
gustatory sense actually can't do without the
olfactory system: without odour perception,
the arousal of the gustatory sense will malfunction.

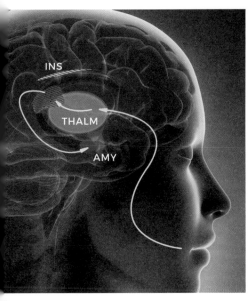

THALM - thalamus, AMY - amygdala, INS - insular cortex (insula)
Taste is transported to the thalamus via
the tongue buds, goes through the area of taste
and ends up in the amygdala.

4.4 AUDITORY ABILITY

Statistically, there are six times as many girls as boys who can keep a tune while singing. Women are also more sensitive to gradations in volume, which might explain why women are more sensitive to differences in volume during commercial breaks. Women are also better able to recognise emotional nuances in a person's voice, such as the 'tone' that a seller strikes while shopping. Women are generally more sensitive to noise. A woman is more likely to get out of bed for a dripping faucet than a man. A man often does not even notice such a background noise (Moir & Jessel, 1991; Underhill, 1999).

In men, the thalamus is likely better able to suppress auditory stimuli due to the male structure of the brain, in which all functions are sharply delineated. The thalamus can filter the transmission of certain stimuli when the cerebral cortex gives this instruction (Bergsma, 2003). Men can completely disregard background noise and sometimes, don't even notice when someone speaks directly to them, as they concentrate while reading. Women, on the other hand, have the ability to divide their attention between different matters and are highly aware of background noise.

4.5 TACTILE SENSITIVITY

It is known that women respond more quickly and more violently to pain than men, although their endurance of long-term pain is greater. During a test performed on a group of young women, it was found that the women were extremely sensitive to pressure exerted on the skin on almost every part of the body. This tactile sensitivity is significantly greater in both young and older females than in males, to the extent that the results of some trials in women did not even overlap the results in men. It appeared that the least sensitive woman possessed a better sense of touch than the most sensitive man (Moir & Jessel, 1991).

Picture above
Noise route: Noise goes up to the thalamus (THALM) into the noise area, through the amygdala (AMY).

Picture below
Tactile route: A tactile stimulus is transported to the thalamus (THALM), via the tactile area in the neocortex and ends in the amygdala (AMY).

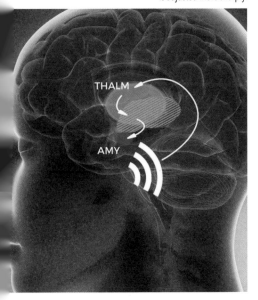

One of the main reasons why women are generally more sensitive than men is because the amygdala is adjusted more sharply.

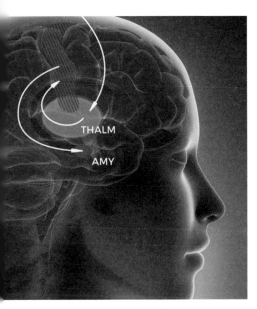

Tactile sense: Women are extremely sensitive to pressure exerted on the skin. The tactile sensation is formed by our four basic elements, namely: pressure, pain, heat and cold. Tickling, for example, is a combination of pain and pressure.

4.6 CONCLUSION

In women, emotions are spread between both cerebral hemispheres (diffuse) and they also have a more highly developed corpus callosum, which allows for an exchange between the left and right cerebral hemispheres. This organisation leads to more balanced and efficient-functioning brains. This masculine difference could be interpreted from a male perspective as 'a woman is a more emotional being'. A man, however, is not capable of making the cognitive left cerebral hemisphere cooperate properly with the affective right cerebral hemisphere. The left and right cerebral hemispheres are more different from each other in the male than in the female, and do not work as well together because there are fewer connections present in the corpus callosum than in women. Men can therefore switch less quickly between the left and right cerebral hemispheres, which is why men often have either a cognitive or affective attitude. Herein lies perhaps an explanation why men more often fall in love with a product and more easily make large purchases (Underhill, 1999).

5. THE NEUROBIOLOGY OF EMOTION

This chapter describes the similarities and differences in interest, perception

and processing of stimuli to emotion. The stimuli that come into the brain through

the senses all follow their own particular route along the limbic system.

Find out how much influence the limbic system exerts on our rational thinking.

5.1 THE NEUROLOGICAL PROCESS OF EMOTION

Emotions are essentially impulses to behaviour. Emotions influence our cognitive brain and the cognitive brain evaluates and determines the output of these emotions. The limbic system is the centre of emotions, and it roughly works as follows: various sensory stimuli such as sight, sound, touch and taste are perceived by our senses and are then transported to the thalamus. The thalamus then passes the information on to the amygdala and the association cortex. The amygdala evaluates the stimuli on their emotional value and the association cortex turns the stimuli into perceptions. Then the amygdala adds an emotional value to it. The higher the emotional value, the greater the influence on the perception. In other words, the amygdala determines to a large extent how much to respond to the perception. The reaction manifests as one of the basic emotions: joy, fear, sadness, anger, surprise or disgust (Franzen & Bouwman, 1999). The emotion of fear towards that which can cause us damage appears to be preprogrammed in primates. Thus sometimes the amygdala responds with fear even when no danger is present. Thus, the emphatic distress for spiders, in women, might be etched in their brains before birth (Sheeve, 2005).

'People who are constantly in a state of happiness are retarded. Someone who is always happy in this life is blind and deaf and amputated'

(Dresselhuis, 2001).

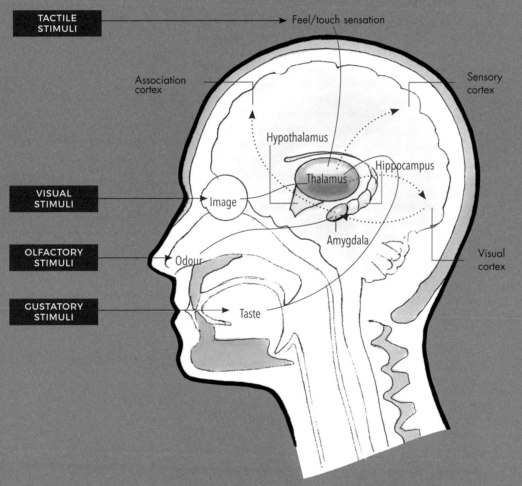

TACTILE STIMULI → Feel/touch sensation

Association cortex

Sensory cortex

Hypothalamus

Thalamus

Hippocampus

VISUAL STIMULI → Image

Amygdala

OLFACTORY STIMULI → Odour

Visual cortex

GUSTATORY STIMULI → Taste

This diagram shows how a visual stimulus enters through the thalamus, is transported to the visual cortex and then, via the amygdala, makes contact with the association cortex and the sensory cortex. These last two assess emotional value.

49

5.2 NEUROLOGICAL PROCESSES IN WOMEN

At a young age, women already have a significantly developed empathic ability. This ability makes them better at recognising primary emotions or mood nuances on the human face, such as happiness, anger, fear, sadness, excitement and boredom. For example, when female babies are brought into contact with other crying babies they are more inclined to weep as well. Women are also better able to read a person's emotional state from their voice (Rozendaal, 2002). Sensory stimuli are clearly experienced more intensely.

Because the corpus callosum is thicker and more convex in women and has a larger number of connections, a greater transfer of information is possible between the two brain hemispheres. Given that the emotional centre in women is located in not only the right, but also the left cerebral hemisphere, where the linguistic area is located, women are better at expressing their emotions and putting these emotions into words. A better developed empathy, however, also has a downside. The ability to perceive a multitude of emotions also means that they perceive more negative emotions than men. As a result, a woman is on average more neurotic than a man. To women, the essence of a successful conversation is the analytical digging. For men, conversation is merely a means to efficiently get from A to B; but women prefer the intellectual challenge of exploring A in depth. The emotion of a woman often thrives on a worrisome image of humanity and the world. Happiness does not make for a fascinating story nor a meaningful discussion (Brunt, 2005).

The same emotions that can lead to greater happiness can also lead to brooding; a closed-circuit thought process in which the negative emotions of undirected anger, fear and negative self-image are expanded by emotion. Thoughts with a negative basis are firmly convinced they are the only thoughts that dare to face the truth. In reality, women interpret a situation more negatively than someone who is optimistic. Women have, due to their greater emotional power, increasingly high expectations of claiming success and happiness. If this happiness fails to occur, they become bitter (Brunt, 2005).

5.3 NEUROLOGICAL PROCESSES IN MEN

Men are less able to express and to put into words their negative emotions. They prefer to keep their negative emotions under control and are more concerned about this feeling lingering around; they prefer to show only positive emotions. Positive emotion in men is often the result of a solution found, a victory or an achievement. In men, emotion is only located in the right brain hemisphere, which less frequently exchanges information with the left hemisphere. Thus, when a man experiences a profound negative emotion, he is

barely able to control this emotion cognitively (the cognitive brain that knows, analyses, thinks, calculates and possesses linguistic skills). The linguistic area in men, unlike in women, is active in both the front and rear left cerebral hemisphere, resulting in a less specialised language ability. This, and the fact that emotion is only situated in the right cerebral hemisphere, means men have a more difficult time articulating their emotions. Therefore, radical negative emotions (in extreme cases) can have a significant impact on men's performance. If the emotions continue unabated, the process can be difficult to stop. Perhaps this explains why men are more inclined to find a solution to a problem before they get into an emotional hold. Neurologically, the communication to the right cerebral hemisphere is temporarily reduced to give priority to the cognitive system. A man then temporarily thinks and acts from the left cerebral hemisphere. Because of this approach, there is also less communication with the limbic system or paleo cortex. The thalamus receives orders from the ventromedial prefrontal cortex (vmPFC, inter alia, which is responsible for inhibition) to suppress certain emotional stimuli. This repression allows for inhibition of the amygdala. In addition, the cingulate cortex is involved, which is responsible for coordination and mediation in conflicts between the results of the limbic system and the neocortex. This probably explains the typical male characteristic of temporarily disabling emotion. Men draw more energy from positive than negative emotions.

5.4 GENERAL EMOTIONAL DIFFERENCES

Men respond more quickly to positive stimuli and draw more energy from them. For example, they laugh more often and more exuberantly in positive circumstances. Men also attach more importance to positive emotions than negative emotions. To them, happiness comes from controlling their environment, scoring a victory, finding a possible or actual solution or reaching an objective (Putrevu, 2001).

Women, on the other hand, smile much more often than men, possibly to indicate that they receive and understand the emotion of another person. This approach probably dates back to prehistoric times. By smiling, those around her were positively impacted, ensuring the safety of herself and her social environment (Moir & Jessel, 1991; Van Putten, 2003).

Women are often more nervous, moody, sullen, gloomy and emotionally less predictable than men. Tensions and emotions, if not too excessive, are more stable in men regarding their physical reactions. Men are better able to perform under heavy mental pressure, knowing perhaps how to temporarily disable or ignore their emotions. A strong focus can, in an extreme degree, also be considered as a form of autism. In women, heavy mental pressure has precisely the opposite effect (Alexander, 1986; Traa, 2005). When the mental pressure is too high in women, their focus falls apart and they can no longer function normally. Women are very dependent on a pleasant prevailing work atmosphere and as a result have less job satisfaction when the atmosphere is not optimal (Leclaire & Zandstra, 2000).

We can conclude that under intense mental pressure, men are inclined to focus strongly on their work (propensity to autism), whereas the focus on work in women declines dramatically and functioning is severely limited (tendency to neuroticism).

AUTISM VS NEUROTICISM

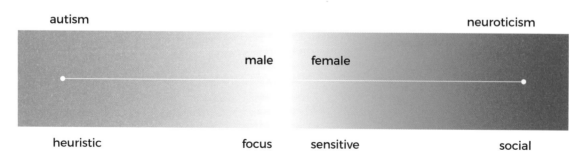

autism   neuroticism

                    male   female

heuristic   focus   sensitive   social

'"...JA. MOOI. MAAK ER NOG MAAR ÉÉN..".'

'...Yes, beautiful. Make another one...'

6. DIFFERENCES IN PRIMARY, SECONDARY AND TERTIARY EMOTIONS

The next chapter covers three types of emotions: primary, secondary and tertiary.

The first emotion arose approximately 200 million years ago as a survival strategy for

a primitive creature. The brain then consisted primarily of a brainstem and a fragile system

that we now know as the limbic system. The word emotion is derived from the Latin *movere*

(moving away). Early emotion was probably not much more than the impetus to move away from

danger. There was a suggestion of a physiological stimulus, but no mimicry or nonverbal

communication.

An example of a primitive
single-celled organism : Amoeba.

6.1 PRIMARY EMOTIONS

In modern people, physiological stimuli engender any of eight primary emotions. These emotions arise spontaneously and automatically in the brainstem without our direct influence. Primary emotions are explicit and require a direct action to respond to the emotional reality of the moment. In addition, a facial expression is a result of an emotion. These primary facial expressions belong, except for small nuances, to the range of universal facial expressions.

6.1.1 JOY-HAPPINESS-GLADNESS

Joy, happiness and gladness are caused by dopamine release from the reward system. Dopamine is sent to a part of the frontal cortex, the nucleus accumbens, and is transmitted via the frontal cortex to other parts of the brain. When this occurs spontaneously, it is called the 'bottom-up reward' or the 'mesolimbic dopamine pathway.' Joy is almost always a spontaneous uncontrolled emotion. Therefore, when we artificially try to generate happiness by acting or faking, there will be virtually no release of happiness hormones.

Joy is for men a performance-oriented emotion. Men see this as a reward after personal achievement or acumen; confirmation that they have managed to get something under control or whether they have enforced happiness.

'Men attribute success to their skills, and their failures to other factors, such as an insufficient effort. Women attribute success to luck and consider a failure to be the (obvious) result of a lack of talent' (Tobias, 1996).

For women, joy is something you share with others. Women see in joy a confirmation that the group or subculture can enjoy something as a whole. Joy works cumulatively for women: the more individuals experiencing joy, the greater the joy she feels. It is striking to see that women at a time like this often seek eye contact with everyone involved. They try to read and absorb the delight on all the various faces.

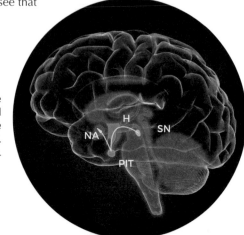

The mesolimbic dopamine pathway runs from the substantia nigra (SN) to the hypothalamus (H). The hypothalamus (H) gives an order to the pituitary gland for a dopamine release. The pituitary gland (PIT) then starts sending dopamine to the nucleus accumbens (NA), a part of the frontal cortex (the reward system). The nucleus accumbens (NA) is settled in the consciousness.

6.1.2 HUMOUR-LAUGHTER-BURST OUT LAUGHTER

Humour is a combination of surprise or amazement and joy. It occurs when logic appears suddenly illogical or when we encounter an absurd situation. The brain is always looking for balance in the left (cognition) and right (affection) hemispheres. However, when a conflict arises between the left and right brain, they collide with each other, in a sense. There is an apparent dissonance between two brain areas involving (1) the septum (a connection between cognitive and affective processes) and an area around the amygdala (organ for emotional assessment); and (2) the nucleus accumbens, which is the reward area and part of the frontal cortex (thinking). Both areas register an error and ask for a review or a correction of the thinking route. The brief clash, conflict or imbalance creates a laugh, laughter or smiles.

Humour is an effective means of relaxing the brain. This mental relaxation has a direct impact on physical health. For example, humour can relieve muscle tension in the body, which is often the cause of headaches and neck or back pain. Laughing also triggers the release of pleasant substances such as dopamine, which provide a refreshing and positive feeling. Humour is the means to overcome the issues of the day and helps to bring things into perspective.

Humour for men is one of the major emotions. For example, men tend to turn a disappointment, sadness or a stressful situation into humour by imagining an absurd fantasy show. This is because they have less ability to express sorrow or to regard it as a useful emotion, and thus they don't give their sorrow attention.

Women can more easily express emotions such as laughing or crying. They experience both emotions as useful and see in both a certain beauty. Women consider a life in which one has only laughed as one-sided and incomplete. For women, humour belongs to one of the many emotions. This explains why women, unlike men, love to watch soap operas in which many emotions are expressed and wherein mostly positive and negative emotions alternate.

6.1.3 FEAR-CONCERN-ANXIETY

Fear is the most pure emotion we have and was one of the first emotions that primitive humans and animals developed. Fear is an emotion that enters into consciousness through our subconscious.
This emotion ensured the survival of primitive life forms by causing them to flee from danger.
Fear is thus a form of automatic protection.
Many forms of anxiety are preprogrammed during the embryonic stage. Behaviour that stems from fear is called conditioned behaviour. The amygdala in our limbic system plays an important role.
The amygdala is a kind of sentry that accurately analyses every incoming signal and assesses its emotional significance. It then sends out signals to the autonomic nervous system (VTA area) where inter alia muscles, facial muscles and the intestinal tract are controlled. Thus, fear stems from past experiences and conditioning, but it can also be caused by ignorance or unknown and strange things. Evolution has probably ensured that it is safer to avoid the unknown. Men and women each posses a different construction of fear.

Men have less fear on average; however, they are more aware of possible threats. Fear can also provoke a certain challenge in men to control and manage it if possible. Men are generally inclined to take more risks. According to psychologist Marvin Zuckerman, this has to do with the brain enzyme monoamine oxidase (MAO). This enzyme creates fear and anxiety in our behaviour. Low levels of MAO, as are found in men, have a calming effect. This lower level of MAO is due to high testosterone

levels inhibiting the production of the enzyme. Low MAO content disposes men to take more risks (Rozendaal, 2002).

Then again, men develop more fear of things they cannot control, such as sickness or suffering from chronic pain. Women rest more easily with these types of unpredictable problems (Moir & Jessel, 1991; Putrevu, 2001).

When a product of a particular brand entails a higher risk, men do not evaluate additional objective sources. Being 'cognitive processors', they less quickly notice small differences in risk. Women do evaluate more subjective and objective sources and in case of an increased risk will base their evaluation strategy on cognitive grounds.

Women, on average, have more forms of anxiety and in a wider area; e.g., anxiety in the form of concerns or the fear of being excluded from a group.
Another form of anxiety is an anxiety disorder or phobia of everything that walks, crawls and flies, such as spiders, beetles, worms and beetle-like insects (Alexander, 1986; Dudlink & Clifford, 1996; Putrevu, 2001).

Paradoxically, women have significantly less recognition of risk than men. I remember a situation where an unknown woman came to me in the middle of the night at a deserted gas station and asked for a lift. During the lift I asked her why she got so easily into an unfamiliar car. Also, in the autumn, when it gets dark earlier I regularly see women on my race bike at abandoned places. I am very aware of the unsafe situation but it always surprises me that women themselves are on the road alone and far from civilisation. Perhaps they feel sufficiently safe at times like this. I know my daughters have no problem in cycling through an unlit forest path during the night.

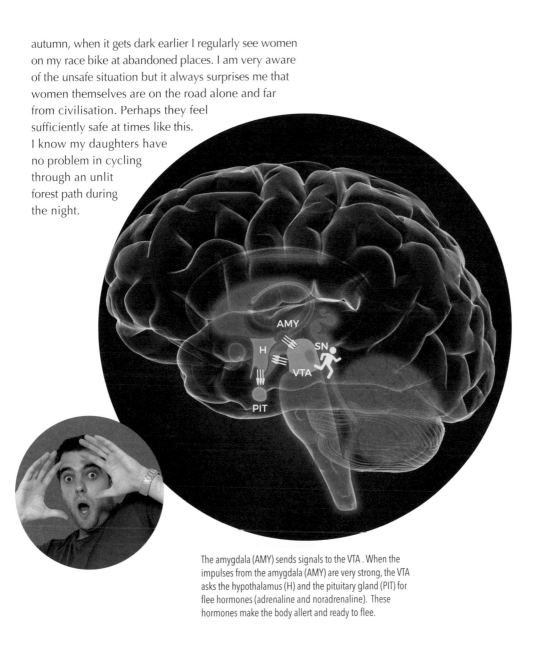

The amygdala (AMY) sends signals to the VTA . When the impulses from the amygdala (AMY) are very strong, the VTA asks the hypothalamus (H) and the pituitary gland (PIT) for flee hormones (adrenaline and noradrenaline). These hormones make the body allert and ready to flee.

6.1.4 ANGER-RAGE-AGGRESSION

Anger, rage and aggression are caused by stress. Rage is actually a combination of disappointment and helplessness. The frontal cortex where the high cognitive functions are located (the front part of the brain) is responsible for filtering or inhibiting our emotions. This inhibition causes us to focus. Under increased stress, it is possible that this inhibition is reduced in the frontal cortex, or even may be lost completely. When the inhibition is reduced, the emotional system takes the upper hand. In men, we often see decreased inhibition in the frontal cortex, probably due to higher testosterone levels, which are responsible for aggression. In terms of anger, men and women do not exhibit the same behaviour.

Male anger manifests itself more in aggression towards his environment. As described above, men have less inhibition in evaluating the complex emotions coming from their environment. If a man is really angry he has a narrower perspective, which frequently degenerates into forms of physical aggression or rage; thus, men more often show direct physical aggression. This kind of aggression is explicit (clearly visible).

Female brain during anger

Male brain during anger

Women, however, have more connections between the left and right hemispheres, which makes for better communication between reason and emotion; they are thus better able keep anger under control. The corpus callosum, which allows these connections, has more capacity to carefully consider reason and emotion so that the acute emotion (anger) is more easily diminished. As opposed to men, women often exhibit indirect (implicit) verbal aggression (Moir & Jessel, 1991).

In the area of domestic violence, women are just as aggressive as men or even slightly moreso (17.6% and 17.52%, respectively). Many studies show that women are also more likely to initiate physical violence. It should be noted that women are more often injured by domestic violence. This percentage of domestic violence is relative: women experience 70% and men 30%. When we look at the total number of victims of violence, according to doctoral research performed in Amsterdam, 60% of those needing first aid and 80% of those requiring ambulances, were men (Richel, 2003).

An article in Elsevier even suggests that over 90% of the perpetrators of violent crimes in various cultures are male and more than 90% of the victims are men as well. Women tend to select as partners tough guys who do not shy away from confrontation. And the knight in shining armour, many women's dream man, is of note because knights spend a good deal of their time fighting (Rozendaal, 2002). This reinforces at least the 'current image' that men are more aggressive than women.

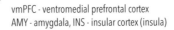

Considerable research has found a direct link between aggression and testosterone. In addition to being responsible for a decreased inhibition (aggression), testosterone is also responsible for the urge to compete, assertiveness, motivation and ambition. The level of testosterone in men is as much as 20 times higher than female testosterone levels. However, in young men, the average testosterone level is highest. In men, the testosterone level performs in a fixed raterhythm, allowing the hormone to reach a peak every six to seven days. Testosterone is highest in the morning, and is approximately 25% lower in the evening. Testosterone also fluctuates during the seasons: it is at its peak around the fall and is at its lowest level in the spring (Moir & Jessel, 1991).

vmPFC - ventromedial prefrontal cortex
AMY - amygdala, INS - insular cortex (insula)

6.1.5 SADNESS-SORROW-SOMBERNESS

Sadness, sorrow or somberness is the result of a combination of incomprehension, impotence and/or a traumatic experience that manifests itself as depression and/or anxiety, which leads to a temporary or long-term dysregulation of the emotional brain and limbic system. This disruption causes reduced levels of endorphins, dopamine, noradrenaline, serotonin and oxytocin hormones. One feels dejected and sees everything as more negative than positive. One fails to relativise certain things and sometimes experiences a flattening of the whole spectrum of emotions.

Men tend to isolate themselves when they are sad, attempting to process the grief himself. This is probably because this emotion is less well supported by his linguistic system, making him less able of putting his grief into words. For a man, grief is a not a harmless neurotic disorder. His emotional capacities are simply less well developed, which in turn causes grief to be evaluated, handled and disposed of less efficiently. Men will attempt to rationalise or relativise sorrow to rid it of as much emotional value as possible; they will frequently try to find a way to minimise or eliminate pain via humour (Moir & Jessel, 1991).

Women are much better equipped to deal with emotions. They seek more support from others (especially of their own sex). This leads directly to an increase in oxytocin levels, which are responsible for solidarity and trust. They evaluate the emotional dimensions of the sorrow, which allows it to diminish. Women also show, on average, less embarrassment when expressing their emotions when it comes to grief or loss (Moir & Jessel, 1991).

6.1.6 AMAZEMENT-SURPRISE-EXCITEMENT

The emotion amazement, surprise or excitement can have two effects, depending on the person.
One person enjoys being surprised and the other becomes insecure or disorganised. It probably has to do with one person having an adventurous nature vs. another type that seeks security. Those who like to be surprised are unconsciously or consciously looking for a dopamine or adrenaline rush. The area of the brain responsible for this reaction is located in the ventral tegmental area (VTA) of the protoreptilian brain (brain4stem). The VTA is the area where many pleasant feelings originate and it plays an important role in motivation, pleasure and intense emotions such as sexuality and addiction. One of the important dopamine pathways originates in the substantia nigra. Dopamine then finds its way to the amygdala (emotional memory) via the hypothalamus to the nucleus accumbens. When dopamine enters the nucleus accumbens (enjoyment area) it enters the consciousness and produces a 'wow' effect.

Men like to be 'surprised' by remarkable things. This probably has to do with the fact that men are more playful and more curious. At a young age, boys need more space than girls. Boys move around much more within their scope, experiment more frequently, and at a young age, it is noticeable that boys need more space than girls. Men are clearly in need of more originality. They love technology and can become enamoured with all sorts of gadgets and novelties in the field of science or engineering (Moir & Jessel,1990; Van Putten, 2003).

Women are more likely to be surprised by signs of commitment to confirm a personal relationship. They are more sensitive to subtle nonverbal cues, such as a smile or a subtle gesture. They seek approval from others and appreciate positive verbal reinforcement. Women are relationship-oriented and like to be surprised with, for example, a small (spontaneous) gift with which they confirm their mutual friendship. Conversely, they like to surprise others by demonstrating great care and dedication, with the aim to develop or strengthen social relationships. In women, a 'surprise' is more often the result of social solidarity. (Putrevu, 2001). Women generally have more affinity with what we call shopping: looking at things, comparing prices, discussing with the staff, asking questions, trying on clothes and eventually deciding to make a purchase. They traditionally buy more than men and are often more pleased with small purchases. They can get excited, for example, by a spectacular sale or the purchase of a unique item at a flea market. A store where everything can be looked at, felt, smelled, and perhaps can be tasted, is a feast for the female senses (Underhill, 1999).

PFC - prefrontal cortex, NA - nucleus accumbens
H - hypothalamus, SN - substantia nigra
VTA - ventral tegmental area, AMY - amygdala

6.1.7 AVERSION-DISGUST-HORROR

Few studies have been published about the emotion of aversion and disgust; therefore, it is still relatively uncharted territory. The insula appears to be involved in basal emotions such as disgust. The insula is a transitional area between the neocortex and the paleocortex (limbic system). It is assumed that this region processes sensory stimuli into a coherent emotion; the insula might play a central role in subjective experiences. Compared with other emotions, it appears that this emotion can be plotted. For example, consider being in love. The love-angel Cupid can point his arrow, out of nowhere, at someone with whom one is infatuated. Infatuation lasts approximately a year, and during this time, other forms will appear to take its place, such as friendship, bonding or shared interests. If this does not happen, the infatuation may disappear. It seems like a power button has been switched off.

Conversely, there are also examples of dislike or disgust that can suddenly turn into an attraction or enthusiasm. Think of a place where it smells like eggs. The smell of eggs can be qualified as an unpleasant odour, whereas it might be viewed at a dinner party as a welcome addition to any dish. There are many examples in which aversion can change to attraction and vice versa.

Psychological studies reveal reasonably convincing evidence that women hold more antipathy than men. Both attraction and disgust appear to be more common in women; however disgust appears more often. Virtually all studies show that women experience more intense likes and dislikes. In other words, women experience things they like with a greater enthusiasm and their distaste borders closer to revulsion and disgust than with men. This greater intensity of reaction may explain the tendency to frequently use adjectives and superlatives such as dingy and dirty but also amazing, sweet and beautiful in their conversation.

Women are also more likely to use language that could be described as rude and impolite. They also refer to more detailed and unsavoury bodily functions and point out unsightly clothing and accessories on any person in general. Discussions about sex, however, are less desirable for women than for men (Alexander, 1986). Women are also more susceptible to encouragement, appreciation and even minor flattery. They welcome support or compliments because they are more often unsure of themselves, and thereby gain more confidence.

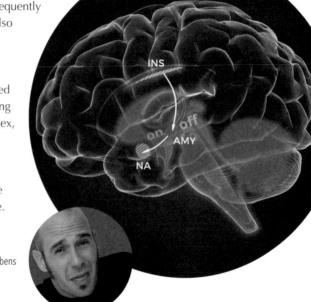

INS - insular cortex (insula), AMY - amygdala, NA - nucleus accumbens

64

Men are not entirely insensitive to flattery, but are more down to earth. They will judge a compliment on its merits and respond with laughter when they receive flattery. In men, flattery can lead to a kind of aversion because they do not particularly appreciate unclear allusions or superfluous compliments (Alexander, 1986).

6.1.8 EMBARRASSMENT-TIMIDITY-SHAME

Embarrassment is caused by an extreme evaluation process of a thought, performed by the frontal cortex and the amygdala, which evaluates emotions. The amygdala sends an extremely negative signal of fear, causing a kind of blockage in the frontal cortex. This blockage has much influence on the area responsible for inhibition (called the ventromedial prefrontal cortex, or vmPFC), which keeps emotions under control. When inhibition is disorganised and temporarily disabled, the emotions govern. The amygdala keeps repeating these fear signals, creating a self-reinforcing system, in other words an overarousal. The fear signals then penetrate into the deeper parts of the brain, such as the VTA area (midbrain) and part of the protoreptilian brain. Panic occurs, the heart rate increases, the body may start sweating or hyperventilate, and a blush on the cheeks appears. The degree depends on the severity, from light shame to panicky embarrassment.

Women are more prone to light panic attacks such as embarrassment and shame. The typical female thought process of frequent reflecting, consideration and weighing of options can lead to this. If it does not take on extreme forms, it can even enhance femininity. Think of the beautiful girl who greets you with a slightly shy smile. A brand or product can, with images like these, express authenticity, transparency, fairness and openness.

In men, a slight, momentary embarrassment can also be disarming for a brand. Think about a tough guy in a convertible who looks shyly into the camera, such as classic movie icons like James Dean or rock 'n roll legend Elvis Presley. The moment of hesitation is very short, but it is precisely the combination of tough with gentle that makes a person approachable in this position.

Shyness is a form of nonverbal communication, which is more original and authentic. It shows some inhibition as compared with the uninhibited, brutal form of materialism. Shyness is chic, delicate, beautiful, artistic and endearing. It shows that a person is aware of his surroundings and his actions.

vmPFC - ventromedial prefrontal cortex, AMY - amygdala, BS - brainstem, MED - medulla

6.2 SECONDARY EMOTIONS

The following secondary emotions are a spontaneous follow-up on the primary emotion or a combination of two primary emotions, based on conation or behavioural intention. In contrast to primary emotions, secondary emotions last longer and have several emotional pathways. For example: someone could be very angry (a primary emotion) but that feeling can fade away in a week. However infatuation (a secondary emotion) can last for a year or more.

6.2.1 PRIDE-HIGH SPIRITEDNESS-HONOUR

Pride is a form of the primary emotion joy. It can be directed towards the self but it can also be directed towards any other person or group. In the case of pride in another person, it is often a person or group with which one is very involved. Pride is frequently an inner joy due to achieving something personal that deserves self-respect, like stopping smoking or completing a course of study. Too much pride can arise from a lack of self-criticism and too little attention to the value of others, and can degenerate into arrogance or excessive belief in their own abilities. However, with shy people, pride can help reduce self-confidence and raise self-esteem.

66

Brands often express their pride through nonverbal persuasive communication, i.e. showing off. With fashion brands, we often see this reflected in a directed imagery or through film. Hereby, models are often depicted from a very low perspective and they look straight ahead or slightly upward. Brands implicitly refer to pride or encourage materialism by promoting pride and self-confidence.

Due to men's higher testosterone levels, they have more confidence than women. They prefer an individual approach and an appeal to personal status such as power, knowledge, expertise and aspects that lead to impressing others. Men are competitive, action-oriented and more explicit in their communication. They reflect more easily to one another the things in which they excel. Men tend to overestimate themselves more quickly. Thus, pride fits men better than women.

Women have more mood swings in which they more often feel insecure. Pride can help women towards greater self-esteem and self-confidence. Due to women's greater empathy and their strong connection with a community, they are more often proud of other people, such as being proud of the kids, proud of their life partner, and so on.

* DOUBLE-JEOPARDY PHENOMENON
Double-jeopardy occurs when a large and a small (niche) brand are equally well-known. Although brand loyalty is equal, the popularity and the purchase frequencies differ, so an apparent difference between the two brands occurs. Big brands achieve slightly more success in terms of buying behaviour, brand loyalty and attitude than small brands as a result of this double-jeopardy effect.

6.2.2 ADMIRATION-REVERENCE-RESPECT

Admiration is a combination of faith, respect, reverence and appreciation and it rises far above liking something. Admiring someone sometimes transcends to great appreciation, causing that one person to be seen with much respect. Admiration arises because someone carries out an extreme performance, is very successful, is highly regarded and has many supporters. Admiration is mainly very useful for young people to get motivated by looking up to someone. It acts as a focal point at one particular position on the social ladder, inviting the admirer to deliver an above-average performance. It works as a sort of 'pot of gold' that appears to be at the end of every rainbow.

When someone displays considerable admiration for an iconic figure, the amygdala (emotions assessed on their value) becomes positively activated. When this occurs repeatedly, the amygdala becomes positively conditioned (for this revered person). The amygdala then gives a signal to the hypothalamus. The amygdala is responsible for emotional behaviour and emotional memory. The hypothalamus is directly connected to the pituitary gland to which it passes on the signal to the amygdala. The pituitary (an endocrine gland) then secretes hormones such as dopamine and endorphins. Endorphins are also known as the happiness hormones and they provide a refreshing and pleasant feeling. Endorphins also provide extra energy, numb the body to pain and make the mind alert. People who enjoy worshipping, meditation, prayer, sex, dancing or socialising experience an endorphin rush. Dopamine creates energy, feelings of joy, sharp concentration and a great motivation to acquire rewards and enjoyment.

The highest goal that a brand can reach is that it is adored. Brands like Apple, Ferrari, Prada and Chanel thereby come close. These brands are intrinsically performance oriented. They invest a significant proportion of their turnover on innovation, technology and/or appearance. Brands like these spend relatively less on advertising because the appearance of the brand itself speaks to the imagination. One also speaks of a double-jeopardy effect*. Less luxurious brands can also be admired because they achieve success in a particular area as an idealistic proposition on the environment or a solution to a social issue. In addition, they can excel in terms of outstanding design and/or innovation and are accessible to a wider audience.

Men have more admiration for brands that have a high level of innovation or are technically advanced. Men are impressed by technical information such as the horsepower, pixels, clock speed and torque capacity or the addition of technical images, maps, bar charts and graphs. They also love sleek functional design such as a Macbook, iPad or iPhone, even in cases where the technique is clearly visible, such as a Harley Davidson or a Bugatti Veyron, where the motor unit is clearly visible.

Women frequently adore fashion and cosmetic brands. They often choose properties as abstract attributes with a subjective character, such a nice smell, a cute shape and vivid colours. They often choose brands that pursue an extreme beauty ideal, often portrayed by female role models that may be unreachable or possess unrealistic proportions. Women are looking for romance and often see themselves differently in the mirror than how they really look. The ideal admirable role model can take on such iconic shapes that some women can be seduced to extreme fashion shapes. This is reflected in botox, extremely short miniskirts, fake nails, fake eyelashes and/or the dyeing of their hair in every conceivable colour.

6.2.3 TRUST-FAITH-HOPE

Trust is the positive result of affective and cognitive processes, which are also called conative processes. These conative processes concern will and behaviour, aspiration and power, such as the buying propensity, the buying plan, usage behaviour and behavioural intention. Many neurological pathways advance the process of building trust. The most important routes will be described here.

Cingulate cortex

The cingulate cortex helps with the learning process in the processing of emotions. Its task is to ratify the processing of positive and negative emotions such as reward and punishment. The neocortex will send information about events requiring an immediate response via the limbic system to the cingulate cortex. The cingulate cortex is associated with spontaneous verbal emotional expressions and is viewed as an outdated version of the neocortex.

Septum pellucidum

Considerations regarding positive and negative feelings are evaluated in the septum, in which previous experiences (knowledge/cognition) are taken into account. The septum acts as a kind of connection station between the cognitive processes (cortex and hippocampus) and the emotional processes (amygdala and hypothalamus).

Lateral habenula

The prefrontal cortex (the consciousness) evaluates the information from the septum and the cingulate cortex, but the lateral habenula (the subconscious) plays an important role in the final decision. The lateral habenula is a brain nucleus (fairly recently discovered) that belongs to the smallest regions in the brain. It is responsible for balancing choices and is indispensable to the ability to make decisions. A positive perception of the product results in confidence in the brand, and trust is an important emotion that serves as an essential foundation that can positively influence all other emotions involved. Trust often results in a positive decision by the habenula.

Emotions are hard to control.
The ratio is always strongly
influenced by emotion. You think with
your heart, not with your head.

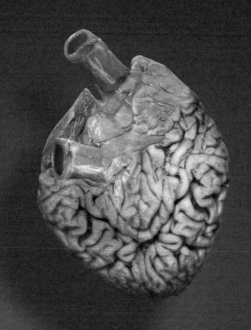

When a brand, based on a longstanding reputation, has built up a relationship of trust, the user becomes less critical of the product. The neurological circuits are conditioned and will often give a positive response regarding the brand. Trust is very important and must be handled with care. When a trusted brand sometimes fails, the user will forgive this rather easily and will put less emphasis on the failure.

In men, the reliability of a product or brand is essential. Compared with women, they place a higher value on quality. Men are also more brand-loyal than women. This probably has its origins in evolutionary biology, in which men were heavily dependent on good and reliable materials to hunt or fight. A sword that was badly forged, for example, may break or may drop from the blade so a fight would be settled quickly. Thus, quality and reliability were often vital. The craftsman entrusted with a commission for a solid product was carefully considered. To ensure optimum quality, guilds were established, in which skills and knowledge were shared, but also games of skill games were conducted, such as archery. Only guild members were competent enough to provide an end product with a brand label. We can now see this as an early instance of a trusted brand.

Women naturally have less interest in technology and possibly in the technical condition of a product. They attach more importance to the aesthetic and emotional significance of a product or material. Women also attach more importance to a relationship or experience of atmosphere around a product, shop or site. They are sensitive to the helpfulness of store personnel and the tips that are provided. Women attach more importance to a close relationship of trust with a favourite site or store. During an attractive and friendly welcome the hormone oxytocin is released, which provides adhesion. An increased oxytocin level also ensures confidence, which makes one more inclined to believe what one is told. A nice package or receiving a few cute samples strengthens the bond of trust with the product. Women love luxury brands when money is not an issue. However, if a similar, less expensive alternative presents itself, they are more inclined to choose it. In that respect, women are less loyal than men. Men are driven to choose the original, and it's also less socially acceptable to go for a copycat brand.

6.2.4 REPROACH-GRIEF-EMPHATIC REJECTION

Reproach is an emotion of unresolved anger. Herein, the septum and the cingulate cortex play an important role. The septum is involved in the regulation of emotions. There are many connections between the septum and the amygdala, the hippocampus, the hypothalamus and the neocortex. It is suspected that the septum serves as a kind of connection between the cognitive processes (cortex and hippocampus), and the emotional processes (amygdala and hypothalamus). Whenever grief enters consciousness, an exchange between the negative emotion (affection) and reason (cognition) will take place. The cingulate cortex divides the area between the neocortex and the limbic system/protoreptilian brain and coordinates and mediates conflicts. The ventral part (belly side) of the anterior cingulate cortex is related to emotional functions and the dorsal part (backside) related to cognitive aspects. It signals stimuli with a reward or punishment character. Because of the resentment, the amygdala generates a negative association that is stored in the hippocampus. When no satisfactory solution arises, the accusation is maintained. Within the brand domain, this often involves the failure of a product or service. It may be, for example, faulty brakes that can suddenly fail, curious or harmful objects in food, networks that interfere or break down during peak usage and all the mischief and damage resulting therefrom. Today we find that brands increasingly avoid inviting reproach, which is in part related to the increasingly litigious culture of a growing number of countries. The transparent world of today ensures that brands must take this into account.

Both men and women store a grievance or accusation in the brain by the same route. However, in women, the emotional and rational considerations will be repeated more often because the corpus callosum, the connection between the left and right brain, contains more connections. In addition, women have a greater need to communicate about unresolved feelings. Reason and emotion are more interconnected. Men will split, process and store something like a reproach as a technically rational and/or emotional issue.

PFC - prefrontal cortex, SP - septum, CG - cingulate cortex
AMY - amygdala, H - hypothalamus, Hip - hippocampus

6.2 5 DESPAIR-DESPERATION-DESPONDENCY

Despair is an emotion from which a brand must remain far away. In total despair, despondency strikes and leaves deep negative emotional traces in the brain. Despair occurs when a brand is faulty on many levels, is nonchalant, has little empathy and is being very passive. For example, an organisation in which bureaucratic processes inhibit the company; in which it has little or minimal market and a weak position in regard to the competition; in which internal structure is formal and official; and in which it has no or a poor crisis plan, letting mistake after mistake occur. Often these are bureaucratically managed companies that are arrogant, formal, official and process-oriented. In addition, they have an underdeveloped internal and external brand image. This kind of company regularly provides products of inferior quality and insufficiently brings positive product characteristics to the buyer's attention.

The brain creates a downward motivational cycle that causes the production of excitatory hormones, such as adrenaline and dopamine, to be inhibited. Negative thoughts about the brand arise, which are etched as long-term memory (temporal lobe), leaving a negative association in the brain during sleep. A brand scheme is a network of associations. A brand is represented in our memories by a network of memory nodes that are in mutual connection with one another. Central to this network is a memory area where the brand is stored. The connection between the central node and the peripheral memory nodes form a network of associations, and is called the 'mental brand diagram'.

In case of desperation or despair about a brand, men will go looking for a better alternative. Men are cognitive thinkers and act on solutions. Even if elements of a product offering do not suffice, they will try to find an alternative. Men are intrinsically interested in technology and will more easily be able to assess the technical aspects of a product. For men, quality is a high priority. However, this high quality requirement sometimes gets in the way when they have to get a job done. Men sometimes overestimate themselves (and their technical abilities) when they engage in a too large a project and barely manage to complete this without specialised help. For example, a major renovation or the restoration of an old house, to the dismay of their partner!

NA - nucleus accumbens, AMY - amygdala, H - hypothalamus, PIT - pituitary gland

Women act differently when confronted with an inferior-quality product. They quickly accept that a product or brand sometimes does not suffice. Women are better at dealing with both positive and negative emotions. Even when a brand leads to despair, they will put up with it longer. Women more frequently address the symptom and less the cause. When a button does not work on a device, they will try to avoid the button by looking for a different way of achieving the same end. Consider the example of a reading light. When the switch is defective, they will use the alternative of the power plug to make the light turn on and off. In short, women often judge products on emotional values rather than thoroughness.

6.2.6 STRESS-TENSION-FLIGHT

Stress increases the activity of the superior temporal sulcus (STS) and is often just the result of thoughts. This causes increased activity of the insula, an area known for the processing/experiencing of internal emotional feelings (Scherder, 2014). Stress consumes energy and causes a release of hormones such as adrenaline and noradrenaline. These substances make the body more alert and prepare the body for flight or fight. The stress hormone cortisol is then released to rebalance the body. Cortisol ensures that this loss of energy is compensated by converting proteins in the muscles into glucose (energy). Cortisol is produced in the adrenal gland. An excess of stress makes for an abundance of cortisol. Cortisol has the side effects of being anti-inflammatory, suppressing the immune system, increasing blood pressure and impairing memory. Negative people also tend to have more white blood cells, a signal of an immune reaction. Brands in the provision of services sometimes cause stress because they rely on many human operations.

Men can function better under peak stress than women. This probably has its origins in evolutionary biology in which men, in stressful situations such as defending and hunting, had to perform under high stress. When men come under pressure, the emotions converge to create a strong focus. However, when women are exposed to severe stress, the opposite happens because the emotions diverge and focus is lost. Women are therefore mentally less equipped to deal with peak stress. On the other hand, women better endure a lesser stress over a longer period, such as the stress that results in a family feud or the stress of prolonged illness.

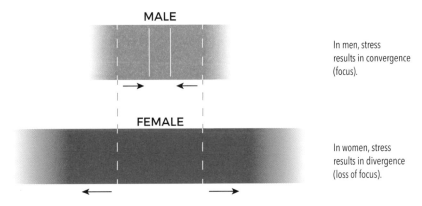

MALE

In men, stress results in convergence (focus).

FEMALE

In women, stress results in divergence (loss of focus).

6.2.7 DISAPPOINTMENT-SHORTFALL-ADVERSITY

When the intended expectations do not come to pass or remain unlikely, one is disappointed. One reason may be that prior expectations have been too high, whereby disappointment occurs. The question then arises why we hold so many high expectations that lead to disappointments. The brain (specifically the nucleus accumbens and the VTA area) appears to make hormones such as dopamine in the expectation of success. This may explain why people like to participate in gambling; the idea alone of winning something makes you happy. People who are prone to experience a thrill will look for activities that cause a short-term reward. The prefrontal cortex, where the nucleus accumbens is seated, weighs only the interest in possible earnings. The limbic system (including the amygdala) considers the probability of possible loss. The brain is mostly focused on short-term profits and therefore will rather go for profit. And when there are opportunities there are losses, which in turn leads to disappointment (Lamme, 2014).

For brands, it is important to not set expectations too high because this can lead to disappointment. Classical disappointments occur frequently in the service category. Consider railway or airline companies that often tout the speed of their vehicles. Telecom companies , for example, can create too many high expectations regarding mobile or Wi-Fi range.

Men are worse at handling disappointment. Thus, men will attempt to avoid disappointment as much as possible by examining the issues in advance and finding solutions. However, thought must be given to preparation on a rational and technical level only. Men are cognitive/linear processors and think in cause and effect until solution. They are more likely to build an alternative route or to carry additional tools, for example. Men accept loss less well, and will therefore prefer to cheat. Because in men the emphasis is on technique, the product must be technically sound in order to avoid disappointment.

Women have less interest in technology, which does not mean that they have no technical understanding. But they often don't develop this technical insight, due to a lack of motivation. Women attach more value to a good relationship and try to prevent disappointment on relational level through an intensive communication with others. For a manufacturer or supplier, therefore, a good relationship with the female consumer is crucial to avoid disappointment. For example, using special wrapping paper or offering free samples, but also by maintaining a relationship through social media.

6.2.8 LOVE-SEX-ENTANGLEMENT

When we cherish feelings of love for someone, the VTA region becomes active. These feelings of love arise because there are many receptors for the neurotransmitter dopamine. Dopamine is a natural drug, which, in the right amount, can provides energy, feelings of joy, sharp concentration and a great motivation to acquire rewards and enjoyment. That is why people in love can have the energy for example, to stay up all night, watch the sun rise, run a marathon or ski down a slope that is steeper than they would normally dare to. Love 'gives wings', makes the mind clear and tempts us to undertake risks (Fisher, 1999).

However, in contrast to love, infatuation is of shorter duration and is maintained for only about one year. After this time, infatuation must become love or attachment; otherwise, it slowly fades away or disappears entirely. Love is one of the most violent emotions that an individual can experience and they may become completely obsessed. It is as if one is riding an emotional rollercoaster. Love is caused by an aggressive cocktail of hormones that the limbic system dominates or occupies.
Intense emotions lead alternately to total happiness, joy, gladness, excitement and desire, followed by anxiety, fear, sadness, depression and anger. Love is therefore an almost unpredictable emotion that also connects totally different individuals. Neurologically seen, falling in love blocks a proper functioning of the frontal cortex. The frontal cortex becomes completely disinhibited, hampering rational thinking and giving emotion the lead.

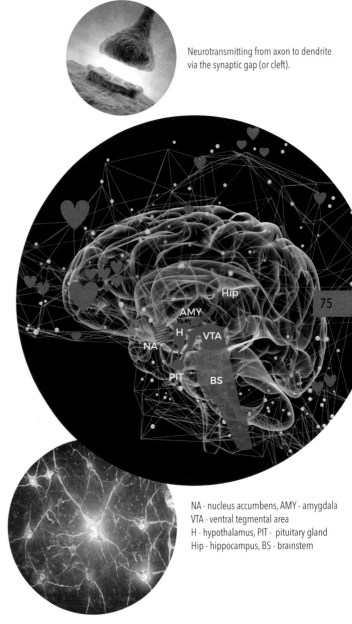

Neurotransmitting from axon to dendrite via the synaptic gap (or cleft).

NA - nucleus accumbens, AMY - amygdala
VTA - ventral tegmental area
H - hypothalamus, PIT - pituitary gland
Hip - hippocampus, BS - brainstem

Our brain contains approximately 100 billion neurons.

This leads to an emotional focus on one person. A salient detail is that the emotion 'disgust' is completely turned off. Reproduction is so important that almost everyone is subject to it. And to prevent everyone running off with the most beautiful girl or boy, a kind of unpredictable cycle of commitments is used in which each individual apparently can be linked to any other individual. Hence the term: 'Love is blind'. However, when the infatuation fades, some totally cannot imagine that they had ever been so in love (Van Raaij, 2010).

Women in this respect are somewhat more susceptible to the 'love' of a husband because they naturally are more romantic. This also has to do with their greater spectrum of emotions. They fantasise about the most romantic situations and are in utter turmoil, able to rave about everything. They can do a spontaneous dance to romantic music, whether with a lamp or a broom. After the period of infatuation they are the ones who take the lead in building a loving relationship. However, when no good relationship is established, they will often be the first to end the relationship.

In contrast, men often fall in love with a woman and sever the relationship less quickly (Moir & Jessel, 1991). In addition, men are also more likely to fall in love with a brand and exhibit more brand loyalty. In other words, the love for a brand develops in the teens, seats itself in adulthood and is unchanged after about the 40th year of life. It is therefore critical for advertisers to build brand preference at a young age. Men are also less price-conscious, make their choice individually and do not consult with their social environment.

It could just be that a man goes out to look for a family car and comes back with a two-seater sports car. They are more likely to choose for themselves at the expense of their families. Women, however, can be in love with a pair of beautiful shoes that turn out to be too small after purchase. In both cases the emotion, over rational thought, determines the choice; however, unlike the man, the woman harms only herself and not her whole family.

For women, the idea, the storyline, the complete picture of a brand is more important than the brand itself. They tend to fall in love with the representation of the product: It's nicely designed, it smells and feels good, it has the right look. She will ask herself: what do my friends think about it, does it summon the right atmosphere for the moment and does it fit into my existing collection? Mind you, women too appreciate the original brand but compromise faster when a substitute at an attractive price is offered.

6.3 TERTIARY EMOTIONS

A tertiary emotion is a phase 3 emotion that results from further consideration. Emotions with a longer duration evolve into a feeling or emotional value. On the basis of evaluation, we develop a specific image or projection. Experiences or influences lead to conclusions.

6.3.1 BONDING-LOVE-ATTACHMENT

Love is unconditional feeling (emotion). Opposed to amorousness, which fades in time, love is a positive long-term feeling. Amorousness ideally leads to love because amorousness lasts only about a year.
In both emotions hormones are produced by the hypothalamus and the pituitary gland such as serotonin, dopamine, endorphins and anandamide. These hormones provide a sense of optimism, energy and feelings of joy. The hormone oxytocin stimulates the sense of belonging. It is released when partners do things together, such as hugging, massage and sex. In addition, these hormones cause people to trust each other more and they are more likely to believe what they are told. The conventional view of love is the classical unity between mother and child, but an unconventional view can be considered for almost everything.
For example, love for sports, animals, art, objects, collections and hobbies. The longer the love for an object, animal or relationship lasts, the more people grow psychologically dependent. The concept of love is closely connected to bonding and attachment, and can be the driving force behind passion, drive and zeal.

Men can have a long-term love relationship for both a partner and friend, but also for lifeless things such as cars, motorcycles, trains, airplanes and other objects. For men, the object itself and the underlying technology are key for the relationship, and the human aspect comes in second. This is why men often have a steady relationship with certain brands.

Women are naturally more romantic and more often dream of a true love or an infinite connectedness. It is they who are constantly working to optimise the relationship and will break it before it leads to nothing. Next to their family, women also build relationships with other things, but always things with a social component, such as horses, dogs, cats, statues or other object, as long a human aspect is involved. Women tend to anthropomorphise objects and animals, for example, by naming their car or ascribing human aspects to it. They are also more likely to value the socio-human aspect of a brand higher than the abstract meaning of the brand itself.

Love - passion

Passion - ardour

Passion - joy

Passion - focus

6.3.2 PASSION-ENTHUSIASM-ARDOUR

Passion is a combination of love, motivation and focus. It is a state in which one is completely absorbed in the moment and forgets oneself, as it were. Passion finds its basis in childhood and has much in common with creativity. The ability to conceive an idea and to elaborate on it is housed in the frontoparietal circuit, which is developed during childhood. The richer a child's environment, for instance in terms of sporty and creative challenges, the better the connections begin to form in the prefrontal lobe (Scherder, 2014).

Passion for something can be energising and can have a contagious effect on others. One is then in a flow that makes the notion of time seem to disappear. During this flow, the nucleus accumbens, also known as the 'pleasure centre', is very active. The nucleus accumbens is a part of the prefrontal cortex and ensures that emotions from the limbic system end up in the consciousness. The amygdala (emotional review) gives positive impulses towards the nucleus accumbens and is thus conditioned and provides impulses to the hypothalamus.

The hypothalamus is heavily involved in emotion and arousal and regulates (among others) blood pressure, heart rate and body temperature. This again makes contact with the pituitary gland which secretes important hormones such as dopamine. This dopamine is a natural drug which, inter alia, plays an important role in love. Dopamine is the drug for enthusiasm and passion and provides energy, feelings of joy, sharp concentration and great motivation.

Passion - flow - love

Passion - motivation

Passion - enthusiasm - energy

© Piotr Zajac

Passion - love - sharpness

Ardour is the experiencing of rewards and enjoyment, which is created by dopamine, and in which the cingulate cortex is involved. Overall, passion is a long-term emotion and forms a kind of 'vicious circle' of happiness. It is known that people with major life goals are more optimistic, build better immunity, are less sick, and therefore live longer.

Men are slightly more prone to completely focusing on something. This has something to do with their biological role in nature, which causes them to have less empathy, and are thus less socially knowledgeable than women. In women, a human presence and atmosphere always play a role; this is somewhat different in men. Men are better able to fully focus on lifeless matter. Hence, many purely technical inventions have been developed by men. For brands, it is a chance to rouse men by introducing them to the technical aspect behind the development of a brand's product. Men thus become enthused, and passion for the brand can be transformed in the brain into a preference for that mark.

In women, it is important for passion to always be combined with psychosocial aspects. Women possess a natural curiosity towards the psychological state, in which interpersonal relationships and social aspects play a role. A brand can generate enthusiasm for their products by paying attention to these aspects.
Women always project themselves towards the environment. Passion originates much more from enthusiasm from the familiar social environment. How do people in my surroundings react to a product when I use it? Women often seek a direct response in which other women play an important role as a kind of role model or checkpoint. Therefore, women are more sensitive to the subjective aspects of a product, such as those that are refreshing, reviving or soft, and terms like trendy and fashionable. Women first evaluate the function (whether or not subjectively) of a product, then the product, then the brand or brand aspects. In men, this order is vice versa. In women, the brand rests at a slightly lower scale, and enthusiasm is primarily due to a product's utility.

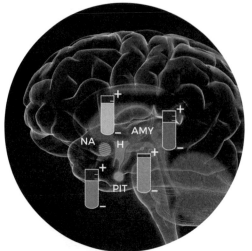

NA - nucleus accumbens, H - hypothalamus
PIT - pituitary gland, AMY - amygdala
When one experience passion, the dopamine levels rise.

6.3.3 JEALOUSY-ENVY

Jealousy often arises from simultaneous (ambivalent) feelings of admiration and envy, from which envy ultimately takes over. To address this issue, we return a few millennia in time. Approximately 10,000 years ago, some crucial changes took place. In this period, our ancestors changed from hunter-gatherers to farmers. This change had many implications for the modern man. The new communities living in a set place had to learn social skills, had to deal with less variety in their food, and were faced with having possessions. It is the ownership of possessions that led to the emotion jealousy. Because one no longer needed to constantly move, one could easily store things. In addition, bartering occurred and money was created. Money and possessions are the breeding ground for jealousy and envy. Whereas it was previously true that if you had something in your hands, it was your own, this had now changed. Successful settlements soon had many valuable possessions and often fell victim to looting. One can imagine the emotions envy and jealousy frequently made themselves felt.

It may sound strange, but there are brands that have based their brand strategy on jealousy. Consider the example of a luxury brand like Porsche. This brand is famous because although less than 5% of the population owns a Porche, 95% value the brand. The individual who owns the Porsche rises in prestige and can sometimes count on a few jealous glances.

Jealousy is not always based on a realistic picture, because the grass is always greener on the other side. Minor jealousy might motivate people to achieve something; however, when something material is unattainable, this more often degenerates in men to looting and robberies. This corresponds to evolutionary biology, in which men held the role as hunter.

Women have better developed emotional abilities, giving them access to a wider range of emotions. This makes them more sensitive and prone to envy and jealousy. Recent research shows that girls more often steal little things, such as cosmetics, which has a significant connection with the primordial role as a collector.

Your garden

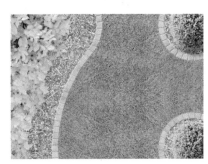

Your neigbour's garden

6.3.4 REGRET-REMORSE-REPENTANCE

Regret, remorse and repentance can arise by introspection: self-observation, self-evaluation and auto-analysis of thoughts and feelings. It is an activity in which one's own thoughts, feelings and memories are made the subject of meditation. Hereby, feelings from the limbic system are analysed by the cerebral cortex. The cingulate cortex is situated exactly between the limbic system and the cerebral cortex and acts as an arbiter because it is involved in the processing of emotions and learning. The cingulate cortex coordinates and mediates between conflicting findings of the lower brain structures and the cerebral cortex. The cingulate cortex only signals stimuli with a reward or punishment character. This process often refers to experiences and events. Reflection is used to better handle similar situations in the future. This function differs little from evaluation.

Brands are made by people for people. In a way, brands are just like people: for brands that go wrong, it is crucial that they respond quickly and thoroughly and, where appropriate, repent. A pre-crisis plan offers the solution. When a pre-crisis plan has been developed, information runs steadily through the media and the hype will soon be nipped in the bud.

Men are more likely to have compassion when a brand repents and then dissolves. Men are rational processors and think in terms of cause, effect and solutions. In short, men fight to resolve a dispute, then drink a beer together and tell each other a joke.

In women, regret is somewhat more complex. They will evaluate the mistake several times from different angles. The responses in the limbic system go on longer and reduce in strength later. Women are a symbol of love and care, but they are also a paradox. Women maintain feuds that can last generations. It is therefore important to give a woman more attention after a brand dispute by perhaps giving or sending her something nice.

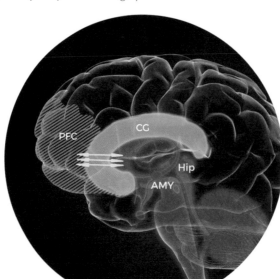

PFC - prefrontal cortex, CG - cingulate cortex
AMY - amygdala, Hip - hippocampus
Regret arises when your feelings do not agree with your cognitive decision.

82

6.3.5 CONTEMPT-CONDESCENSION-DISDAIN

Contempt is a combination of overconfidence, lack of interest and lack of introspection and can be described as the tendency to form a fast and unfounded judgment. It often is caused by a reluctance to delve into something, and this is reflected in superficiality. Superficiality is caused by a number of short, unfinished routes in the brain that work to get to a consideration faster. The consideration is actually too short, causing emotion to play an important role in the final judgment. It is like judging an elephant on his swimming skills.

Within the brand domain, contempt arises from indifference to its own brand/product and the user. The producer discovered a basic need that could be exploited commercially. Gain is the starting point, and the product or service is marketed as quickly as possible without a thorough investigation.
The short-term goals are being served and there is no attention for the welfare of the customers. No real relationship is established with the audience. Sometimes, raw materials are knowingly processed that can be harmful to the environment or to humans. There is frequently trust on a vast group of consumers, and a small group of critics is ignored. These critics often watch helplessly.

In this respect, men belong most to the group of short-term thinkers. They are competition- and prestige-oriented and also have a smaller spectrum of emotions at their disposal. The competitive drive is due to increased testosterone levels on which the structure of men's brain is built. Men are agentic

(self-organising) processors and have a linear thinking pattern that focuses on solution-oriented action.
Within the theory of evolution, a human life was short and survival and reproduction very important. The role of the man was very focused on opportunity, in which success was more important than the long-term consequences. The end often justified the means.

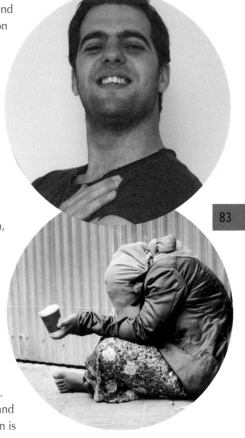

The brain of women is, in comparison with men, much more balanced in weighing a goal and its causes. A decision is considered much more often in various ways in advance so there are as few victims to be made as possible. Disregard is generally less common in women. However, competition and contempt among women is more common.

6.3.6 INDIFFERENCE-NUMBNESS-DISTANCE

Indifference is a combination of an accrued or arisen contempt, numbness and disinterest. Indifference is an emotion with the least arousal response or a minimal emotional activation. It is caused by a multitude of disappointments or a childhood in which the environment was not challenging enough, yielding fewer incentives. Indifference is more common in people with a higher EQ, IQ and FQ: emotional intelligence, cognitive intelligence and motor predisposition. Individuals with this higher development naturally need more incentives to develop these qualities. It is therefore essential for a certain type of brand to take this into account. These include a brand with a particular body of knowledge to be transferred in order to convey the product features clearly and carefully.
In addition, it is necessary that an brand actively communicates with its audience by transferring the right incentives with regard to the product.
When this does not happen enough, the audience may become bored and develop a certain disinterest in the brand, which is frequently due to communicative incompetence or disinterest in the brand itself.
The user may be facing disappointment after disappointment and thereby become negatively conditioned about a brand or company.

Every brand consists of a field of brand associations. Every encounter with the brand adds positive or negative assocations. These are then stored in the temporal lobe, where the long-term memory resides. Other parts such as the hypocampus and amygdala are active during the storage as well. The brand association field is not a passive but an active area (Van Raaij, 2010).

It should be clear that indifference in respect to a product or brand is disadvantageous, for both men and women, for a good brand relationship.
For a brand, it is therefore crucial that indifference never occurs. Men need more incentives in this regard than women. Especially during childhood, boys are very physically active and sensitive to external stimuli. The vmPFC area in the prefrontal cortex where the inhibition of emotion is located, is completed at a later time in boys than in girls. Men reach adulthood therefore at a somewhat later age, but the inhibition will always be less tightly adjusted than in women.

In women, there are other aspects that may cause indifference about a product or brand. Indifference covers the entire limbic area, where the emotion and the brand are nested. The nucleus accumbens plays a key role in activation of a brand in the prefrontal cortex. The ventromedial prefrontal cortex is located in the same area (vmPFC area), which is responsible for the inhibition. By indifference to a particular brand, it is important that the limbic system is activated extra without activating the vmPFC area. In women, there is another form of inhibition in the vmPFC area. They will step less spontaneously into the spotlight, but are less inhibited about bodily issues. Thus, it's important to pay sufficient attention to optimising their beauty or eliminating their ailments. If insufficient attention is given to one of these cases, attention in general or disappointments can lead to the development of a certain indifference with respect to a brand or company.

Indifference can also be due to a medical cause. The lateral habenula (decision area) is responsible for weighing choices. When it is damaged or disabled, one becomes indifferent to choices.

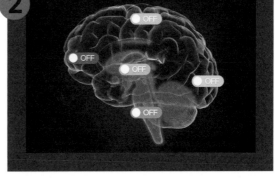

FIGURE 1: Research and development department
FIGURE 2: Neuro shutdown
FIGURE 3: The customer

6.3.7 HATRED-IMPLACABILITY-RANCOUR

Hatred arises from an unresolved conflict, a humiliation or a conviction. One can perhaps only hate someone with whom you have a relationship. Which one is indifferent, one cannot hate. The emotion hatred, as illogical as it may sound, is subject to a paradox of love. One can hate someone with whom they have an alternating good or bad relationship; a kind of love/hate relationship. The cingulate cortex, hippocampus and amygdala play an important role. The cingulate cortex is seen as a primitive neocortex which arbitrates between the neocortex, where the higher cognitive functions are located, and the limbic system, which houses emotion. The primary job of the cingulate cortex is to make decisions about reward or punishment regarding right or wrong behaviour. The amygdala has due to feelings of hatred generated a negative association that is stored in the hippocampus.

There are many products with which we have a love/hate relationship, such as unhealthy snacks, cigarettes, alcohol, drugs or other personal products. Sometimes a brand deliberately chooses to sharply position itself with lovers and haters because they carry a very distinct product and do not want to compromise.

Both men and women are familiar with feelings of hatred. Men tend to look for confrontation or ignore it. They are the ones who often choose very distinct products or services. Men develop somewhat less resentment than women but male actions lead more often to hatred.

Women are emotional creatures and more often develop hate or love. They experience things they like with a greater enthusiasm and their distaste borders closer to hatred and disgust than men. This greater intensity may explain the tendency to use more adjectives and superlatives in their conversation.

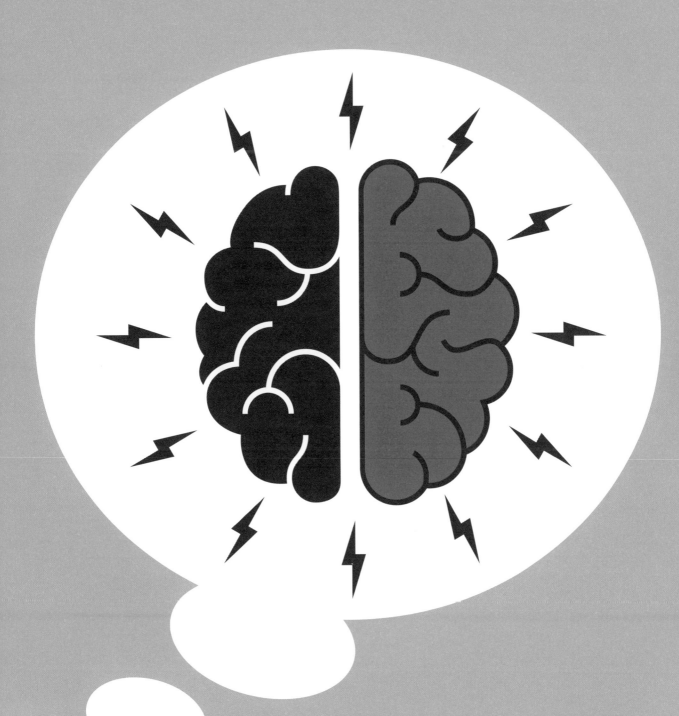

6.3.8 IRRITATION-ANGER-RESENTMENT

Irritation is an emotion that can lead to anger. Irritation causes negative thoughts that lead to stress. Negativity takes energy, which causes a release of hormones, such as adrenaline, which make the body more alert. When there are negative thoughts the amygdala and the hippocampus are involved. If the irritation is of temporary duration, the stress hormone cortisol will bring the body back to the status quo. When the stress is longer, negative thoughts can be transported from the hippocampus (short-term memory) to the long-term memory. An irritation that settles in the long-term memory is difficult to turn back into a positive bias for a brand. A positive experience is passed word of mouth, but a bad experience is often on the tongue. The basic brain systems respond more often to negative than positive experiences. Positive things need little control but negative experiences can be harmful to the surrender. Our brain is mostly an old system that applies laws that millions of years ago were considered the best solution. For the brand, it is crucial to cause as little irritation as possible with consumers and when it does happen to reduce this as quickly as possible. Many brands have come up with a standard solution to resolve complaints quickly and give gifts as compensation. For both men and women, the emotion 'irritation' follows the same pathway in the brain; however, women experience positive and negative emotions more intensely than men. In addition, women need more time to forget negative emotions. For some brands or services a good alternative is not available, so one should take for granted the irritation. In these cases, we see that women can more easily put the situation to rest.

6.4 CONCLUSION

CONCLUSIONS REGARDING WOMEN

Unlike men, women have a symmetrically organised brain. The female brain works better using both brain hemispheres, whereby they have a broader spectrum of emotions at their disposal than men. Therefore, they may perceive sensory stimuli as more sophisticated and intense. In woman are both positive and negative emotions effectively.

CONCLUSIONS REGARDING MEN

Men have by nature a greater sense of humour because this emotion is generally better to keep under control and is easier to handle. Persuasive communication based on humour works more efficiently and more effectively on the psyches of men because men appreciate the value of positive stimuli more.

7. GENERAL IMPLICATIONS

This chapter describes the implications the theory from the previous

chapters has on persuasive communication in general.

Various points that further explain and substantiate the differences

between men and women will be addressed.

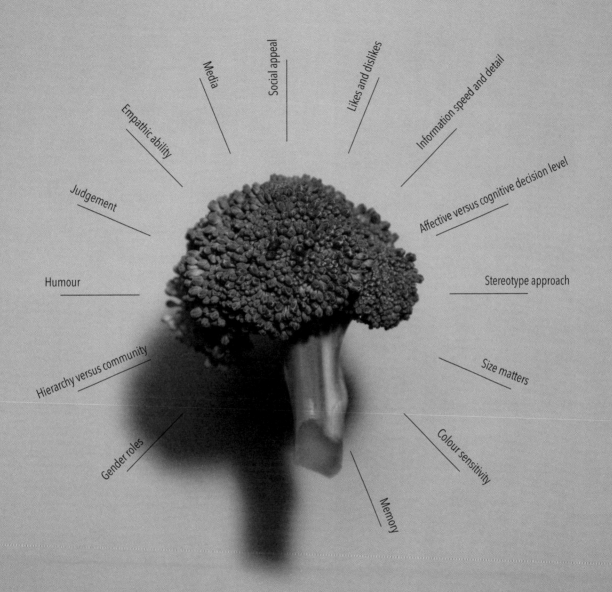

Media

Social appeal

Likes and dislikes

Empathic ability

Information speed and detail

Judgement

Affective versus cognitive decision level

Humour

Stereotype approach

91

Hierarchy versus community

Size matters

Colour sensitivity

Gender roles

Memory

7.1 INFORMATION SPEED AND DETAIL

Please read this text, it only takes 1,16 minutes!

`00:00` Men are quicker to absorb offered information such as an advertisement. This is probably because they observe and process information that is fragmentised into main issues. `00:07` These main issues often consist of arguments, characteristics and attributes of a brand, product or service. `00:11` Women need more time than men to form a reasoned judgment because they want to absorb all the detailed information. `00:29` Unlike men, women pay attention to things such as fine colour gradations, captions and any human emotions. When a woman wants to receive an ad message quickly, she more often limits herself to only the visual language or the total atmosphere (Alexander, 1986; Van Putten, 2003; Hupfer, 2002). `00:50`

By incorporating more time for information processing, brands could take more account of women. `00:54` For example, using visual and/or spatial presentations both in stores and at trade shows. Such situations increase the need for women to assess the product (e.g. food) through multiple senses (touch, smell, sight) (Underhill, 1999). `01:16`

Rituals is a great example of a store/brand that incorporates time for information processing. Women can smell and try out all kinds of products. 'Happiness can be found in the smallest of things. It is our passion to transform your everyday routines into more meaningful rituals' (Rituals, 2000).

7.2 AFFECTIVE VERSUS COGNITIVE DECISION LEVEL

Men base their opinion more often based on cognition. At the same time, men are less able to switch between the left and right hemispheres. This means that in the selection process they often react either completely rationally or emotionally. Brands could anticipate this by convincing a man first through cognitive arguments and then afterwards affectively.

Take, for example, the purchase of a particular car brand. If a man rationalises his choice on a cognitive level, he can then be influenced emotionally. Cognitive issues about a high price will usually be suppressed because he mainly decides on emotional grounds. Rationality is temporary in the background or is completely unavailable. Men prefer cognitive decision-making that only later will be substantiated or supported by affection. The emotional brain in men is linguistically less supported; therefore, they are less able to put emotions into words or name them. Decisions that are made purely from the right cerebral hemisphere (emotional part), bringing him thereby to (total) confusion because there is little cognitive support. This confusion can lead him to love a particular type of car, and infatuation often leads to less critical buying behaviour.

Men choose for themselves rather than for their social environment. The decision-making of a man is based on choosing brands that confer status, and men are more brand loyal than women.

Men are also more likely to fall in love with a woman and less likely to break up a relationship (Moir & Jessel 1991).

Women sense much more because emotion and rationality, via the left and right cerebral hemisphere, are in constant contact with each other. They collect various materials, relativize, think back and thereby make their choices. As a result, they more frequently doubt whether they should purchase something or not. Women are also more sensitive to atmosphere and search for more confirmation of their decision. These complex mental machinations may make a woman more uncertain; therefore, they often play it safe, which could be a pitfall.

93

AGENCY: CARMICHAEL LYNCH, MINNEAPOLIS
'The more kids you have, the more practical it becomes.'

AGENCY: BLAHBLAHISM, AMSTERDAM, CLIENT: CAPI EUROPE
It is not stereotypical to use a male model as a sex symbol in advertising aimed at women. Only a perfect, tasteful execution will be effective on the female audience. One example is the execution of the Capi Europe campaign.

7.3 STEREOTYPE APPROACH

Although culture differs by country, the gender roles of men and women have a major influence on local advertising; much advertising is still very stereotypical. For example, the man is often portrayed as giving guidance and the woman plays a dependent role. It is mainly women who quickly see through false emotions. Most advertising does not appeal to female logic and is therefore not credible. According to neurological principles, it is much more effective in advertising to reverse the roles. Women are more inclined to daydream and fantasise, and they like the image of a sensitive and considerate type of guy. For example, they like

a man who clearly pronounces his feelings, who listens understandingly and who confirms his expressed feelings/characteristics that are associated more with the feminine domain.
On the other hand, it is sometimes also interesting to show male characteristics in women; e.g., women who can easily separate side issues from essentials, who show more confidence and who aim straight for their goals. This reflects the mirror neurons of both sexes, whereby we face ourselves.
In everything we experience, the self is supreme. We are always first with ourselves. Such a strategy will impact both sexes.

94

Man: 'So I have a big butt.'

Woman: 'I'll have one those man burgers.'
Voice-over: 'Ok, since you want to act like men so much, we'll act like women.'

Man: 'Honey, does my butt look big in this?'

Woman: 'No, not really.'
Man: 'So it does.'
Woman: 'No it doesn't.'

Woman: 'Not at all, you have a beautiful butt.'

Man: 'And why didn't you say that?'
Woman: 'But I just said that.'

Man: 'Yeah, when I ask you. Never mind, this is going to be another fun weekend.'

Voice-over: 'The big big Mac, a man burger, so for men and for women that still want to try it now.'

AGENCY: DDB & TRIBAL, AMSTERDAM
According to neurological principles, it is much more effective in advertising to reverse the classic gender roles.

7.4 HIERARCHY VERSUS COMMUNITY

Men form teams and see the world they live in as a hierarchy in which they flawlessly find their place. If the man with the dominant position is clear, the other men accept this and are in solidarity with each other. However, when the opportunity presents itself, men rather grab for power and try to gain control. Men are thus sensitive to power.

Women see the world more like one or more communities to which they may have something to contribute or where they can find connection. They are more focused on finding balance in the community than hierarchy. Women can develop themselves better in a mixed gender workplace than among women only. However, when there is no choice and they have to cooperate with each other, something like a 'hierarchical system' occurs, in which they struggle longer and more intensely for a place.

Men in such a situation find and accept their place more quickly. They are also more in solidarity with each other in a working relationship. Women are sensitive creatures and therefore are not always nice to each other. Women observe each other to a far greater extent and are much meaner when it comes to a conflict. Women will wonder rather 'how will I prevail and how should I approach my rival to achieve this'. This pugnacity perhaps stems from evolutionary psychology, in which women were sometimes forced to survive in a community where they struggled to fit in.

At a brand level, one should appeal to a man's power, status and his feeling of being able to impress others; women are more sensitive to the approval of others and connection within the group (Moir & Jessel, 1991; Hupfer, 2002).

7.5 SOCIAL APPEAL

Many psychological experiments have shown that women are more interested in social contacts, and there is evidence that these social contacts are maintained more intensively. This evidence is based on the careful research of behavioural scientists, studies in the field of preferred newspaper topics and analysis of conversation fragments overheard by scientists. In one of these studies, in which conversations were recorded and studied, 37% of women's conversations were about individuals, compared with only 16% for men. Another similar study showed 51% for women, compared with 27% for men (Alexander, 1986).

Women have a wider view of the world in which human intuition plays a central role. A feminine society is less materialistic and addresses the social aspects more. Women prefer 'real people', including their strong and vulnerable characteristics. Women possess greater empathy and are therefore better able to empathise with others. They are superior in interpreting nonverbal stimuli (analogue communication) such as posture, facial expression, smells and sounds. Women study the eyes, facial expressions and the complexion of people. There they can infer emotion, atmosphere and mood. Women also have a superior visual memory that makes them capable of remembering external detail in clothing combinations and accessories. They are also intrinsically interested in others, take into account the feelings of the other person and want to know what others think. Women pursue common goals and seek connection and kinship in their social environment, in which they prefer to live on equal footing. They draw more energy from encouragement, seek the approval of others more frequently and want to know often how others deal with certain situations. Women compare themselves to other women, which is why women like to look at men as well as other women.

The biological characteristics of a man are hardly influenced by cultural influences. This means that the deepest instincts of men (such as aggression) are the same everywhere and cannot be changed. Therefore it is important to take this into account in advertising. When, for example, a male model in an advertisement looks straight into the camera, it can generate a certain degree of rivalry within the male viewer. Lingering eye contact between men can lead instinctively to aggression. Consider the many incidents in which (especially young) men for whatever reason bump up against each other in a nightclub. When there is eye contact for too long in such situations, this can lead to aggression on both sides. There is still a kind of pack behaviour present in male evolution, wherein dominance plays an important role. When the power relation is not clear at any given time, there may be a tendency towards conflict. The example discussed here comes from empirical research and is often taken into account in professional practice.

Whereas eye contact can generate rivalry and aggression between men, eye contact between men and women is an important part of the dating ritual, in which the woman is decisive. A man only gets to make eye contact when the woman want to.

The man can then take the initiative. Men often think that they themselves are responsible for the first contact with a woman, but a woman uses her frequent eye contact even before a man is aware of it.

This eye contact is often associated with other non-verbal stimuli, such as eye contact combined with a shy smile; consciously passing closely by him while making eye contact or sharing moments of hilarity where they laugh and make eye contact. The frequency and the length of the eye contact are of great importance. Women have an innate talent for this. Men are primarily visually oriented, and mainly scan salient issues. The approach of a man is often plain and explicit. Women's use of makeup, such as extra rouge, lip gloss or accentuated eyes have an immediate effect. Herein perhaps lies proof that men have less empathy. They often do not notice subtle non-verbal cues, which is why more salient signs need to be communicated and should be repeated.

Experiments have shown that both men and women are more attracted to a person whose eye pupils are larger than in the same situation with small pupils. Just the size of a pupil is, in fact, a primitive form of (non-verbal) communication.

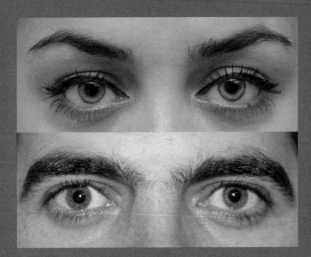

Eyes with large pupils

Eyes with small pupils

7.6 SIZE MATTERS

When exaggerating, one could say that when things increase in size, they are more attractive to men. When things reduce in size, they are more attractive to women. This theory might not be applicable for car brands. Small cars are better to control for women because of their less developed spatial ability. The nose of such a vehicle should be as short as possible in order to prevent the driver's seat being pushed too far forward (Alexander, 1986; Moir & Jessel, 1991). Women often drive smaller cars, but it must be noted that women feel safer in a larger car such as an SUV.

Women also tend to reduce or sweeten up everything linguistically, such as wearing a cute shirt. Little things just look more adorable to women and invite them to be pamperers. I can still picture a situation where a mother held a baby romper in front of her with extended arms and said, 'What a cute baby romper. So adorable!'

In certain circumstances, the above is a marketing tool to take into account. A small ad with a cute handbag will receive more attention from women and a huge ad with a greatly enlarged beer will draw more attention from men.

7.7 COLOUR SENSITIVITY

In the Netherlands, approximately 1 in 12 men (8.3%) have a colour disorder (also known as anomalous trichromats). The most common colour disorder is the perception of the colours red and green. In women, this colour disorder is much smaller and appears in only 1 in 200 (0.5%) women (Brettel, Vienot & Mollon, 2004). Ads aimed at men, therefore, should take into account that men cannot always detect the correct colours. This is especially true when it comes to the perception of subtle colour nuances.

Women have a wider spectrum of emotions and are therefore likely to vary and experiment more with colours; not only in experiments with various clothing styles, but also in grooming and in the many variations in hair colour. Women literally think much more in terms of colour and often take the lead in decorating and furnishing a house.

Because men often have a colour disorder, contrasts and bright colours are often more easily seen. Therefore, men tend to choose more sharp contrasts such as black and white or black in combination with a bright yellow colour. For men, colours can reinforce their identity and their sporty lifestyle. Action, speed and sports: the world in which men like to be. Therefore, men often choose saturated colours, colours that radiate a lot of energy.

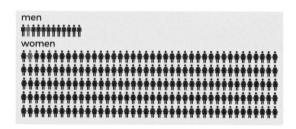

7.8 LIKES AND DISLIKES

READ THIS NOW YOU PIECE OF SHIT!

Women experience attraction and aversion much more intensely than men because their empathy and antipathy are more developed. Communication aimed at women should therefore contain high empathic content; praise and glory matched against blame and dislike. These findings also suggest that it is desirable to develop sales arguments for women based on addressing the issues they do not like.

Advertising aimed at men, on the other hand, is more effective when it is based on the things they do like. These observations also highlight the need for tasteful communication to affect women; an approach that is less essential for men. Advertising filled with crude and blunt lyrics or that directly focuses on bodily functions tends to alienate rather than connect with women (Alexander, 1986).

7.9 MEMORY

Women appear to have an excellent memory for words, facts and visual details; in particular, with regard to written material or useless calls in certain radio programs. This is likely due to the fact that women have a better-developed left cerebral hemisphere, where the linguistic area (in women at one location and limited) is situated (Alexander, 1986). Women are able, at least for a brief period, to store more irrelevant, incoherent information in their memory (Moir & Jessel, 1991). I still remember the performances of my two little daughters in leotards, who effortlessly performed complex steps and movements for my wife and I.

Men appear to have a better memory for geometric figures or observed forms and memorising distances, numbers, dimensions, graphics and designs. There is also some evidence that men, over a wide range of media, can remember written material better than the details of a product when they were presented at a visual examination (Alexander, 1986). The memory of a man is better if the information is organised in a coherent form or has specific meaning (Moir & Jessel, 1991).

When a man explains directions to another man, it will commonly sound like 'Take a right on the first street and take the second left,' et cetera. Women often confuse left and right, which is why directions with landmarks work better for women, such as, 'At the mill turn right, head towards a bar, then towards the playground.'

7.10 HUMOUR

Humour is an emotion that can work effectively on both sexes. Because men have a narrower range of emotions, misunderstood emotions will be grouped under the category humour. Typical examples are subtle and sad situations that require a reasonably developed empathy. Women are more able to analyse such situations and to put them into words so that equal situations are not always perceived as humourous.

In men, humour in advertising can be used much more frequently. They often laugh at the most absurd situations. This is probably because for men, humour is the first subconscious reaction. Men laugh at men and even at the grief of other men. The whole gradation of humour just works better on men. Male grief is also socially rather tolerated as a form of humour.Consider the stereotypical films and comics in which a man is assaulted by a woman. Mostly it is a scrawny man standing beside a big fat woman, preferably with a rolling pin in her hand. Nobody will laugh at that image in reverse. Humour (and aggression) is probably an emotion that men show more easily than other emotions (Brunt, 2005).

Humour among women is much more complex than humour among men. In women, humour may be more wrapped up in a story. The topics addressed in men are much more general. Men dare to speak out more towards each other. A joke about breasts can be more easily made between men than between women. For women, such a topic frequently has a wider, deeper and personal meaning. During the first meeting, for example, two men can entertain each other with humorous remarks or jokes. Men will also laugh more often in such a first encounter. Women are much more tringent during a first meeting and share more mutual information. Something like: the tone of voice, a single word, comma or intonation can have many meanings. I will explain this using the following joke. A man meets another man in a cave

7.11 MEDIA

Women are interested in media containing personal information or tips. Women follow vloggers, bloggers that suit their lifestyle and posts on social media like Facebook, Pinterest, Instagram et cetera. You often see them search for special dishes to cook via an online channel like YouTube and watch the step-by-step preparation. They enjoy the personal contact of an online cook and love to exchange experiences about new dishes, ingredients and kitchen tools with each other. In addition, women frequently use online media to gather a wealth of information about specific products and read reviews of others about this product.

Magazines are still read, but are more strictly selected based on special interests and depth of interest/things that play an important role in everyday life. This often requires more text, which is less accessible via an image on the Internet. Sometimes women just like to relax by sitting on the couch with their feet up while browsing through a magazine.

Media aimed at women are full of women. It seems obvious that they prefer to look at women over men. Women play important role models for each other that they want to imitate. The future is a mecca to sensory experiences. We will be able to zoom in on each detail of a garment, determine our favourite stitching and style, to fit and judge clothing in a virtual mirror, visit a store in every city of the world through the oculus rift and receive every order within a few hours or print it ourselves with a 3D printer.

Women constantly switch between online and offline. It is therefore necessary that these media opportunities do not try to compete but complement each other. As discussed above, each media type has its own power. New features and technologies such as virtual reality, big data, the Internet of Things, just in time 3-D, on-demand and so on will all be a momentary hype, but in the end all will find their own place in the needs and attention of the consumer. Because nobody wants to watch 3D movies all the time, have a virtual reality experience everywhere or never visit an offline store again.

In men, information requirements are less personal and more mass media. They more often visit online news/opinion sites and other media where objective information is available. Men are less likely to subscribe, for example, to a computer magazine or a car magazine. Many magazines are therefore sold in individual sales. Men are very focused on data and embracing new technologies. Therefore, they assess innovations in the beginning more on technique than on content. For men, a symbiosis between online and offline is very successful; for example, the Layer app which offers the possibility to watch an additional YouTube movie via a mobile phone or tablet while reading. Conversely, men should have the oppurtunity to bash an online fly while reading an online newspaper.

© Barone Firenze

7.12 GENDER ROLES

Even though we try to keep from separating male from female tasks as much as possible, we fall back into the classic gender roles unnoticed, again and again. Perhaps both sexes have, without realising, a different role and predisposition. The male role, for example, is divided into father, husband and professional. At work, the decision to purchase a computer system will be entirely different from that of a father of two children. In the workplace, there is a much more rational view of things, such as the capabilities of the computer, depreciation, solidity and reliability. In the role of father, in the purchase of a mobile phone, tablet or computer a man will take into account more subjective things, such as if the child has certain preferences concerning colour, brand, storage or speed.

The female role is often divided into mother, wife, and working mother, and in addition: attractive woman. A great example wherein the different needs of a woman are beautifully translated is in a commercial of Oil of Olay, in which a middle-aged woman is featured. In this ad, the roles of caring mother and attractive woman translated quite nicely. It is beautifully communicated that a mother, in addition to her caring tasks, may pamper herself with beautiful cosmetic products to look good. Herein, two representations are united in one advertising message. Superb! (De Jong, 2005).

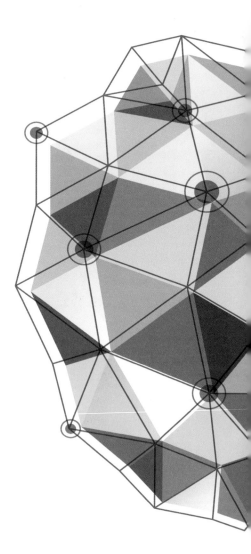

The various female roles

The female empathic ability

7.13 EMPATHIC ABILITY

Women have more empathy, which is why they are better at emphathising with others. They will notice subtle details in facial expressions faster than men. They sooner notice when someone is feeling under the weather, is feeling uncomfortable or is insecure. These insights are not always explainable and often come from pure intuition. Women seem to be able to practically scan a person and just know. Women are emotion-oriented, are very sensitive to the prevailing atmosphere and are very people-driven. This means that every product and/or service should contain something human. When a human emotion is not directly visible, they create emotions themselves. Consider the emoticons used during a Whatsapp conversation or adding feelings to a subject.

Women's senses are also more sensitive and better developed. They see subtler shades, smell spoiled food faster, notice sudden noise levels sooner, are more sensitive to temperature changes, notice a light touch sooner, have a wider field of view, hear better subtle tones of voices, notice weird insects more quickly, more often feel unclean or sloppy, collect pictures of beloved animals, acquaintances and family and surround themselves with all kinds of emotionally associated decorations. Women do not always perceive this as an advantage. The lack of empathy in men makes it easier for them to choose for themselves. Women sometimes long for this independent thinking, which makes them sometimes envy the uncomplicated way men act. Consider the sense of responsibility that the average working woman has for her family.

7.14 JUDGEMENT

Emotion plays a dominant role in the selection process. Prior to the selection process different emotional pathways are followed in men and women. I want to stress that both routes almost entirely take place in the subconscious and which the limbic system is often dominant. In men, those seem to take place independent of each other more often. The following paragraph describes the two main (dopamine) routes, the mesocortical (cognitive impressionable) and the mesolimbic (affective) route.

Men follow two mental paths when coming to a decision. The mesocortical and the mesolimbic pathway. In men, the emotion and reason are more separated. There are fewer connections between the left and right hemispheres which is why a decision, as well as the the selection process, is primarily formed and/or takes place in the left 'or' right part of the brain Men carefully plan when making a decision regarding to something rational such as a tool or

a piece of clothing. They often inform themselves via multiple sources, both online and offline. They decide beforehand what they are looking for, and usually find guidance through a website or shop where a selection of different brands is provided. A utensil for example, requires the man to go through a cognitive process and consider both its price and its quality. Based on those two factors, a decision will eventually be made. In this example, the man follows the mesocortical path; the so-called 'top-down' circuit. In this circuit, the fontal cortex

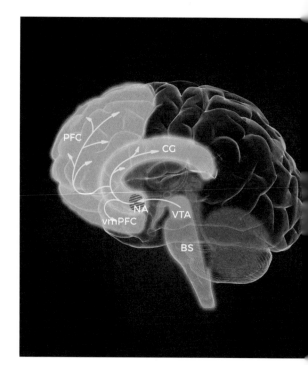

MESOCORTIAL PATHWAY
vmPFC - ventromedial prefrontal cortex, PFC - prefrontal cortex, CG - cingulate cortex, NA - nucleus accumbens, BS - brainstem, VTA - ventral tegmental area

provokes the emotional part of the brain and guides it in a cognitive manner. A man might be more easily influenced by a certain brand, but his choice is usually based on rational factors. For a product to impress a man, it should fulfil certain requirements he has from the start. When these requirements correspond with the buyer's initial image, he will then buy the product. With products or services that carry a strong expressive value, such as cars, motors, shoes, sporting goods, watches, gadgets or exclusive membership, the unconscious mesolimbic circuit is

deployed. In this circuit, affective values (psychological values) play an important role, such as 'What does this mean for my surroundings?' or 'What does this mean for the way people perceive me?' The mesolimbic also influences the regulation of emotional behaviour. In this, the limbic system, and especially the amygdala (emotional judgement) carries the upper hand. The emotional/mesolimbic circuit (the 'bottom-up' circuit) ignites in the tegmentum (brainstem) and projects the information via the thalamus (the switch centre and part of the limbic system) via the ventral part of the striatum to the nucleus accumbens (the pleasure centre). From there, the information goes to the cingulate cortex, which plays a big role when deciding whether something is positive or negative. The cingulate cortex (also called the old cortex) is seen as the forerunner of the neocortex and functions as a kind of mediator between the neocortex and the limbic system. In addition, the lateral habenula (decision region) is involved.

MESOLIMBIC PATHWAY
CG - cingulate cortex, NA - nucleus accumbens
BS - brainstem, VTA - ventral tegmental area

The habenula, a brain nucleus that belongs to the smallest parts of our brain, is probably responsible for comparing decisions and is irreplaceable for making decisions. When a man is emotionally convinced, it is difficult for him to make a rational decision. This also means that men are more sensitive to brands and are less price conscious.

The female brain uses almost simultaneously the mesocortical and mesolimbic pathways when coming to a decision. This is a subconscious process. Women's decision making is more in balance, because there are more connections between the left and right brain, where the cognition (ratio) and affection (emotion) are located. This allows them to communicate better. The corpus callosum, which ensures connection, is broader with women. In addition, the emotional part is present in both parts of the brain. A woman acts mostly from affective processes in which cognitive processes always plays a role. During grocery shopping, they pay attention to the quality or they might critique vegetables or fruits on various levels, such as its ripeness, colour, smell, texture, size, expiration date and cost. This requires more time to do the grocery shopping, but women generally buy food of higher quality.

Even when serious decisions have to be made, such as those concerning investments, women are at an advantage. In these cases, we can also see more balanced decisions on both a rational as well as an emotional level. Women are also more prepared to seek guidance from others before making a decision. We can conclude that women make more

thought-through decisions. It should be noted, however, that a more developed connection between both brain parts can sometimes be confusing. This makes women less capable of separating feelings from facts. Women, therefore, pay more attention to the latest trends and aesthetic aspects are of essential value, such as the properties of colour, smell and detail. When, for example, a certain colour is trending, it will have a big impact on the decision.

An example of when emotions take control over rational decisions is when women tend to make small purchases when they are not feeling well or are unhappy. They consider the purchases as small gifts for themselves, or quick satisfaction.
Such a purchase can be a towel for the bathroom, a pair of earrings or a small ring, items that are not necessarily required. Such purchases often are made in moments of stress, with a desire for a short distraction, such as some alone time. Men do not suffer from this type of behaviour (Wolff, 2005).

Another reason for emotions to take control is the fact that women sometimes find themselves to be emotionally unbalanced, which may lead to them feeling lonely, which could result in the desire to make small purchases to pamper themselves (Wolff, 2005).

7.15 CONCLUSION

Based on these theories, one might suggest that women are superior at making thought-out decisions. Carefully processed and perceived information can be seen as more successful and could lead to a better evaluation or judgement. On the other side are the men, who will, once their interest has been provoked, completely focus themselves on one specific part/subject and gain profound knowledge of that specific subject/part. Men are more cognitive processors; their brain functions happen more in one place, which is more effective than a brain that spreads its functions throughout, the latter being the case with women. When a certain issue requires a specific cognitive approach, for example, a really mathematical or spatial approach, men have the advantage. It should be noted that knowledge of very specific issues rarely occurs in everyday life. Because of this, women will often more make well-thought-out decisions. Eventually, every decision is dependent on the specific processing of information, which sometimes might be to the advantage of men but probably more often to women. This will eventually lead to a superior judgement, and is dependent on the informational characteristics that a message carries.

8. IMPLICATIONS FOR ADVERTISING

This chapter describes the implications the theory from the previous chapters

has on specific persuasive communication in advertising.

This section creates the first handles that will link to chapter 9,

where existing advertising is dissected using neurobiological knowledge.

CLIENT: DAF, THE NETHERLANDS
A rare ad from the famous Dutch car brand DAF
from the mid 70's, which no longer exists.

8.1 LAYOUT

Men prefer a simple layout, straight to the point and focused on one topic. The theme should preferably be captured in a single image, together with a short description in the form of one or two features (Putrevu, 2001). Men also prefer dynamic layouts with lots of action and the use of bright colours (Alexander, 1986). A layout with lots of detail quickly meets a threshold and is therefore less accessible. For men, a layout should be uncluttered and functional. They scan a layout for essentials and therefore spend relatively less time on it (Meyers-Levy & Sternthal, 1991).

Women prefer an accessible and attractive layout. They often prefer more details in an advertisement. Women take in the whole picture, including captions and additional photos. They are more interested in the story within a given layout, in which subjective details, handwritten captions and colour shades give extra meaning. They may be better able to notice two or more messages in an ad and to find a connection.

However, for both sexes, an advertisement should not contain too much information and should be relatively simple in design. A simple and clear advertisement works faster and more effectively with both sexes.

AGENCY: VOSCH THE BRAND GUIDE, OISTERWIJK
'Urban jungle' (Notice the tongue-shaped crack in the asphalt. Men prefer a simple layout, straight to the point and focused on one topic.)

Feeding your cat's instincts whiskas

AGENCY: BBDO, LONDON
Women are more interested in the story within a given layout, they may be better able to notice two or more messages in an ad and to find a connection.

8.2 THE SIZE OF AN AD

The format of an advertisement has a greater influence on men than on women. Men will perceive a large advertisement as important because it strengthens the dominance of the subject. Although a large ad has more impact on both sexes, women will pay more attention when it contains more information. Small ads and web banners are less well perceived by men. This effect is enhanced even more negatively when a small banner contains too much detailed information or is surrounded by other banners. This is different from an editorial webpage, in which a banner is not surrounded by other banners. Women have the advantage in this case, because they are better able to scan seemingly incoherent information, such as many banners together, and judge them on their merits and content. Women analyse an advertisement or webpage more in detail and therefore become less rapidly confused by the number of messages. Generally speaking, an advert aimed at a woman can be smaller in size and can also contain more detailed information.

AGENCY: BLAHBLAHISM, AMSTERDAM, CLIENT: CAPI EUROPE
A large ad has more impact on both sexes.

AGENCY: AMV BBDO, LONDON
Men are inspired by texts with references
that have the achievement of success
as a goal and that are linked to a certain
degree of dominance or control over their
environment.

8.3 THE USE OF COPY

Copy aimed at women is more effective when it is based on literature, art, body care and interpersonal relationships. They are also more sensitive to encouragement, appreciation and even mild flattery. Men are not immune to flattery but are often too objective to appreciate it. Men quickly feel a kind of disgust because they recognise it as perhaps disingenuous (Alexander, 1986).

Women participate more in the storyline and tend to experience the story from their own perspective, based on home, friendships and feelings (Moir & Jessel, 1990). Thereby, women are more susceptible to an exact and precise choice of words because they have greater facility with linguistic matters and read text easily. Therefore, it is important that copy aimed at women is more precise compared to copy for men. The wrong choice of words can quickly inspire a negative feeling in women. Copy aimed at men should carefully explain what is meant. It might even be advisable to use more words for men and perhaps, to repeat important information in different ways because a word has less meaning for a man (Alexander, 1986; Putrevu, 2001). Women understand a communication message more quickly. They probably have more aptitude for it, and women probably find it more fun to follow advertisements (Wolff, 2005). Although statistical facts often have a powerful effect on men, for women such facts are generally less convincing or are even confusing. If it is necessary to mention statistical facts, it is wise to support such facts for women with descriptions of what is being shown and to include a picture of 'an authority' in this area (Alexander, 1986; Putrevu, 2001). Women study information more extensively than men, even when there is little attention value provided by the information. This does not mean that all information evokes attention. Poorly observable information is less noticed by both men and women. The fact that women take in more extensive and detailed information also means that they can be influenced more easily (Meyers-Levy & Sternthal, 1991).

Men will pick up a story (based on a social subject) with more difficulty. They may have trouble understanding it or will not be able to confirm it for themselves. If it is not immediately clear what the ad is about, they quit trying to understand it. Men are attracted to texts based on appearance and personality. Men are more independent, self-centred and competition-focused. They are inspired by texts with references that have the achievement of success as a goal and that are linked to a certain degree of dominance or control over their environment (Putrevu, 2001). Men often use a more adventurous vocabulary than women (Moir & Jessel, 1991).

Large chunks of text will not be read by either men or women. Texts should be short and to the point. Texts must also be credible and contain realistic promises. Stories with unrealistic claims such as 'When you have a headache, you cannot take care of your family' or promises such as 'With this potion you can be who you want to be,' etc. do not work in today's society. Credibility has become more important, although there are possible nuances between men and women (Wolff, 2005).

It's lonely at the top, but at least there's something to read.

The Economist

8.4 TYPOGRAPHY

AGENCY: REVOLUTION BRASIL, SÃO PAULO

For women, the font used in combination with the image is of great importance. They pay more attention to subtle details of a styled font and its decorative possibilities.

AGENCY: TONIC INTERNATIONAL, DUBAI

Men more like surprising and original fonts that stress the contents of the image, or a new and unique combination of letters.

For women, the originality of the font is of less importance. They attach more importance to the atmosphere of the overall picture and less on the rationale behind it. Women pay more attention to subtle details of a styled font and its decorative possibilities. For women, the font used in combination with the image is of great importance. They take in all the detailed information and try to interpret the overall feeling of the image. Women notice subtle details more quickly, such as differences in line distances (more white in typography), font size or the correct use of punctuation. Texts may also contain colour or subtle nuances to clarify the text content.

For men, typography has primarily a functional value whereby the overall picture should radiate a certain peace (or dynamic). Men think more in terms of clear contrasts in which one moment creates total peace and in another situation creates the opposite. In both cases, men would rather not be distracted by explicit typography when it adds nothing. Men are certainly interested in special fonts, but only if there is a clear reason for them. They prefer, in specific situations, dynamic letterforms, perspective and alignment of the font. Men respond more quickly to large and prominent headings with an original punchline. In short, men more like surprising and original fonts that stress the contents of the image, or a new and unique combination of letters (Van Putten, 2003).

8.5 USE OF COLOUR

Women are clearly at an advantage regarding colour recognition. They recognise colour sooner and can identify it more accurately. When an appeal is made to men with colour in advertising, it is better that the colour is actually shown. However for women it is often sufficient to just mention the name of the colour. Moreover, for both sexes showing the colour communicates more effectively. Men often find it unclear when there are only words about a colour in online and offline advertising, or via radio. Men will, in many cases, not understand what the ad is about (Alexander, 1986).

Men prefer chromatic (saturated) colours or clear black and white contrasts. This is probably because they distinguish subtle nuances less well. That is not to say, of course, that the use of achromatic (unsaturated) colours is undesirable.

Women have a greater sense of colour harmony and their use of colour is more flexible and diverse, because they can distinguish subtle nuances exquisitely. Warm colours draw women's attention and symbolise the message. Women prefer warm grey over cool grey, while in men, it is just the opposite. Creative professionals can benefit from this by freely using shadows and shades in promotional materials for women (Alexander, 1986; Khouw, 1998).

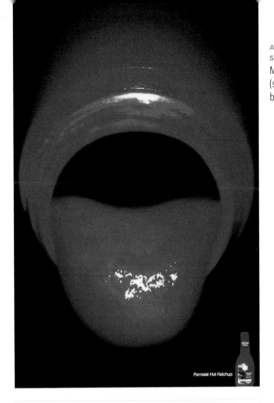

AGENCY: DM9 DDB, SÃO PAULO
Men prefer chromatic (saturated) colours or clear black and white contrasts.

119

AGENCY: DÉBUT ART, ARNO, LONDON
Women can distinguish subtle nuances exquisitely.

8.6 DESIGN

Women appear to naturally have a greater sense of aesthetics. Their sophisticated perception leads to more attention to detail. Women can generally perceive colours more accurately and better distinguish subtle colour nuances. They have a better sense of proportion in terms of colour and structure and dare to experiment more with colours and shapes. Designs intended for women should include subtle details and emotions, in colour as well in the human aspects. Women are able to take in and process many different details. Furthermore, designs can be very romantic and evoke emotions from the past, such as retro influences from the film and fashion industry.

Men are generally more creative and inventive. Their childhood fantasy world develops itself far into adulthood. 'In men you often see the little boy' (Dresselhuis, as cited in Camps, 2001).
Men have a superior sense of spatial proportions, they can rotate intangible objects in their minds. They strive more to symmetry and seek peace in a design, which often manifests itself in large areas of colour with high contrast. Men often choose saturated colours and dynamic designs. They love action, that translates into controversial angles and perspectives. Men possess an inimitable passion for technology and like to see that reflected in a subtle way in design. Design intended for men, although dynamic, must remain clear. This means that an advertisement with many dynamic elements must not look cluttered. Men primarily assess salient details and clear contrasts. There should not be too many subtle shades of colour next to each other because men often have difficulty assessing exact colours (especially the colour spectrum from red and green), subtle colour shades and soft shadows (Alexander, 1986).

AGENCY: DDB, MADRID
Women are able to take in and process many different details.

AGENCY: SAATCHI & SAATCHI, LYON, CLIENT: TOYOTA
Design intended for men, although dynamic, must remain clear.
This means that an advertisement with many dynamic elements must not look cluttered.

8.7 MEMORY OF BRANDING

Many memory tests reveal that men have a better developed memory for names and slogans, even if in hindsight they proved fictitious and were designed for short-term use. This characteristic has its origins in prehistoric times, when the choice of weapon was vital. A weapon was chosen for solid material that was reliable and made of quality materials. The maker of the weapon (the blacksmith) represented a certain brand value. The master sign of the blacksmith in the metal can therefore be seen as an early brand mark or logo. The specific choice of a particular weapon is now reflected in the choice and preference for a particular brand. In addition to a preference for quality, men often opt for a brand to emphasise their status. Perhaps that explains why men are more brand loyal than women, and also less cost conscious.

Women often remember the symbolism, the corresponding feeling that is evoked by a communication message and product characteristics. When different brands have the same product characteristics, the brand is less important. Women look more to the product itself and thus are more likely to opt for a substitute.

It is worth noting that men in general remember an original advertisement better than women. This applies to all parts of the communication message except the imagery (Alexander, 1986).

AGENCY: JUNG VON MATT, ALSTER HAMBURG
Men are better at remembering names, slogans and design characteristics.

AGENCY: UNILEVER, ROTTERDAM
Women often remember the symbolism, like this beer used for this detergent brand.

8.8 COMPLEXITY OF THE COMMUNICATION MESSAGE

Women aspire colourful advertising with many supporting photos or illustrations complemented with small captions. The ad may be colourful, because women think a lot more about colour. The female brain is better prepared to handle complex communication. A woman is better able to extract relevant data from incoherent information. Women have a superior visual memory regarding detailed perception, with the exception of written information. They can easily switch between various components of a communication message, such as text, captions, visuals, photographic details, colours, melodies and smells.

Advertising for men should focus on one issue and one clear visual. For men, colour is less important. They think more in terms of instrumental value (functional information) and ability, the number of cylinders, and characteristics like top speed. Men are less equipped to process complex information. They are more likely to review the information on some key issues, and therefore will instead try to sort the information into a simpler whole. A man is a cognitive, (agentic) processor and he tries to process information mainly from facts. Men can, in contrast to women, remember written information better than, for example, the visual detail of a product.

AGENCY: LEO BURNETT, LONDON
Advertising for men should focus on one issue and one clear visual.

AGENCY: PUBLICIS, AMSTERDAM
Women aspire colourful advertising with many supporting photos or illustrations complemented with small captions.

'Men are usually more direct and want to be approached more directly. They make less effort when there is a detour to understanding. Men prefer to be direct and stick to the point. They prefer communication without a detour and no complex wording. Women are born organisers. They are more proactive and know better how to manage complexity. A woman always thinks ahead while a man apparently lives in the moment' (Wolff, 2005).

8.9 SOCIAL ASPECTS IN ADVERTISING

Women are, unlike men, community oriented. The human/social aspect of advertising is therefore of great importance to women. This human aspect could be an attractive man, an attractive woman, an animal or even an object in which human traits are visible.

The greater time women spend on social contacts is important to take into account in the development of products that play a role in social life. Women look for humanity in the brand. Advertising should be based more on social life and especially on individuals who are either celebrities or fictional persons (Alexander, 1986).

If there is such a thing as a personal feminine endeavour, then women prefer attractive models that exude happiness. This feminine endeavour can be described as attaining often unrealistic ideals of beauty, ultimate happiness, romantic life or a role as an attractive seductress. Women allow themselves be fooled about this. They might prefer living the illusion of achieving these goals, as it provides them with an ideal image of life. In short, the use of attractive models is more effective when the models give the idea that the 'idealised dream world' is within reach.

However, the use of models for women is much more complex than that. In addition to the fact that women love looking at attractive men and women, they also like to look at real, perhaps less perfect humans.

Because of their high empathy, they can empathise with the mood of the model and view the model's visible emotion. They study the eyes, facial expressions and facial colour. All these facets of emotions are very interesting to women and can provoke various reactions. For example, an image of a disadvantaged husband or children inspires the caring, helping nature of a woman.

Men are cognitive processors and for them it makes no difference whether or not a human aspect is present in a communication message. They react with as much emotion about people as about objects. In many cases, this means that showing a product in a specific setting could be sufficient for brands aimed at men.

When there is nevertheless a male model used, a man prefers a model with a male appearance. A man identifies himself easiest with a confident, tough-guy model (Moir & Jessel, 1990). However, it should be borne in mind that misuse of a male model can induce rivalry. In some cases, it is not desirable to use a male model since this can be perceived as threatening and inspire aggression in certain situations, such as direct eye contact between the male model and the male viewer. The setting has a major impact and should be evaluated carefully.

In contrast, a man prefers direct eye contact with a woman and the use of a female model can actually be very effective (Moir & Jessel,1990).

This is because, as described earlier, the woman determines the contact with the man, for the most part. It should be noted that a female model can also distract attention from the brand. This has to be applied very strictly. The feminine charms themselves distract but may serve very well, for example, in challenging a man to choose a particular brand and type. Women can appeal to achieving success, status, independence or power. Men are agentic and competitive and they rapidly accept (perhaps one-sided) competition.

Women understand a message presented by a human that is grafted into a storyline more often than their male counterparts do. Women often find it more interesting to actually keep track of a story and probably are more gifted at that than men. Men have more trouble with this kind of communication. They usually do not understand the hidden meaning within a story (or simply refused to acknowledge it). Men often find issues that are not rational stupid or exaggerated. They refuse to comply or simply turn their heads away because they cannot empathise to the same degree as women. Women are much more emotional and have a caring and soft side, that is evident. They consider the possible consequences more than men do: when and what could go wrong?

AGENCY: ALMAP BBDO, SÃO PAULO
Women can empathise with the mood of the model and view the model's visible emotion.

AGENCY: PROXIMITY BBDO, BANGKOK
Men react with as much emotion about people as about objects.

8.10 HEURISTIC VERSUS COMMUNAL

Men are transformational when it comes to choosing. As cognitive processors, they reach the essence of a message step-by-step. From cause to effect to objective evidence. Their actions are often carried out in order to reach a certain goal. This approach makes men more competitive and makes them value status more. Men think in a limited manner and focus on one single matter. Social aspects play an insignificant role during the thought process of men. Men as subjects of a single specific processing unit will value a message that is focused on only one quality a lot more than women will (Putrevu, 2001).

Women are social creatures in whom the human is the centre. They care less for the technical side of a product and more for the information on its actual working process. This is why it is necessary to provide women with enough information regarding the possibilities, organisation, accessories, usage and maintenance of a product.

AGENCY: LEO BURNETT, LONDON
Men are more competitive and value status more. Their actions are often carried out in order to reach a certain goal.

CLIENT: L'OREAL
Women are social creatures in whom the human is the centre. They care less for the technical side of a product and more for the information on its actual working process.

AGENCY: GUTE WERBUNG, HAMBURG
Men have always been interested in the big idea. It is important to have a clear concept incorporated in the message.

8.11 CONCEPTUAL ADVERTISING

Men are naturally more playful, active, sporty, experimental, and they care about research. They often show more interest in the backstory of something than the actual story itself. This is why men have always been interested in a possible 'catch'. It is important to have a clear concept incorporated in the message.

Women are usually looking for one or multiple storylines that contain various emotional components within a commercial message. A woman values ideal beauty, whilst men are aware of the fact that clearly a lot has been manipulated during retouching. Women are more aware of interpersonal relations, such as a social issue and its total experience. The concept, the big idea, whereas the finding or the catch are of less importance.

AGENCY: GREY, TORONTO
Women ar more aware of inter-humane relations such as a social issue and its total experience.

8.12 AGENTIC VS. COMMUNAL

Advertising for a male audience is more effective when it appeals to personal qualities such as security and independence. The person themself usually is the centre with men, in terms of motivation and interests. These characteristics are classified as something personally oriented that is also known as agentic oriented. Joseph, Markus and Tafaodi's research in 1992 has shown that men remember information better when it's personal, and that women remember information much better when it concerns someone else. The manner in which males form judgement is often based on analytic and logical connections.

Advertising to a female audience is more effective when it focuses on their identity and personal relations. Not only do they put themselves at the centre, but also their social surroundings. They value personal involvement and harmony within their own environment. Women usually develop a self-image that is mainly based on the important considerations of others. According to Markus and Oyserman, these differences imply decisions, information and a difference in mental processes. Her process, which is focused on others, is also partly connected to her own considerations. These connecting processes that women possess might have to do with the more complex repetition of interpersonal information. This would mean that women are better at

remembering information about others. There is little empirical evidence that it has to do with gender differences and the type of memory one can have. However, in a study on facial recognition, it became clear that women are far superior at recognising faces than men (Hupfer, 2002).

Women usually feel more responsible for their family. When both a man and woman are being held responsible for getting home on time to take care of their children, a man will question his responsibility more easily and choose an important meeting over the care of children. In that perspective, a woman is often more a giver than a taker. She is better at organising her own social surroundings and therefore feels more responsible. Of course, the necessity of nurturing and guilt also play a role to a certain degree. Women do not like to give away their nurturing role because they feel everything needs to be done properly and feel as if they can do a better job, which is why they will take up such tasks rather than giving them away. Men are not always trusted with nurturing tasks. Women feel as if men lack the social side and that they perceive nurturing as a task to be solved with simplicity. Men are too formal and lack sensitivity in these circumstances.

AGENCY: SPRINGER & JACOBY WERBUNG, HAMBURG
'Freedom since 1933'
Women usually feel more
responsible for their family.

9. CASE EXAMPLES

In this chapter, we will discuss several ads, based on the previously described theory.

These ads were selected from a range of international ads. Many of these were nominated

and/or received awards, which indicates their high quality; in some cases, however, these ads

are less effective for the targeted sex. Poorly made ads are virtually ineffective on many levels

and will therefore not be discussed.

9.1 ADS UNSUITABLE FOR MEN

FORD PUMA CAR AD

At first sight, this ad spread seems sufficient. The double-page format has a dominant presence within the magazine and covers the entire field of view so that the viewer's attention is not distracted. This fact is important because men, unlike women, can generally only concentrate on a single task at the same time. The layout exudes calmness and focusses on a single subject. The use of colour is restrained, and the image is dynamic. However, the ad's heading makes the ad ineffective for men. The copy idea is based on humour, which is an excellent approach for men. However, men tend to appreciate the joke rather than the underlying message.

A negative approach is less effective for men. Being overweight and being bald undermines a men's self-confidence. Men desire power and status and want to impress others (Moir & Jessel, 1990; Hupfer, 2002). The ad suggested that a man does not have to be rich; however, men often associate material wealth with success. Being successful is an intrinsic value for men. Men are also competitive and derive a large part of their self-worth from their (material) success. In short, men do not want to associate themselves with a car brand aimed at fat and bald men who have not been successful enough to, for example, afford a Porsche, no matter how beautiful, fast and competitively priced the car in the ad might be (Wolff, 2005).

	negative	neutral	positive
focus on one topic			●
organised layout			●
positive approach	●		
use of colour			●
original idea		●	
action element			●
humour	●		
emotion	●		
appeal to status	●		
size of ad			●

A DRIVER'S DREAM

New 1.7 litre 16V Zetec SE engine with Variable Cam Timing. Delivering over 85% of peak torque from just 1500 revs. 125 HP. 0 to 60 mph in 8.8 seconds. Just 9.7 litres of urban fuel consumption. 4-channel ABS Eletronic System. Extra wide 195/50 VR tyres. The first Ford to be totally designed by a computer. Tested by Jackie Stewart. Puma. Everything you expect from a real sports car. Excluding the price.

YOU DON'T NEED TO BE FAT, BALD AND RICH TO HAVE A SPORTS CAR. FAT AND BALD IS ENOUGH.

AGENCY: YOUNG & RUBICAM (Y&R), MADRID

AMSTEL BEER AD

This ad for the Amstel brand does not fit many of the criteria for the male target group.
First, the ad does not stand out from the rest due to the excessive detail. Men have more difficulty processing complex information and sometimes do not want to understand it (Wolff, 2005). They are inclined to assess information on certain key issues and are more likely to arrange the information to arrive at a simpler conclusion. This is not an easy task for this ad because it has no obvious main theme.

Men also have a more limited range of emotions, unlike women, and are less able to understand all the subtle human interactions in the ad or derive meaning from them. This is probably because men's emotions are less well supported by the linguistic system, leaving a man with only limited abilities to put his emotion into words (Moir & Jessel, 1990).

The colours used are also suboptimal for men, given that approximately 1 in 12 men (8.3%) has a colour vision disorder. The most common colour vision disorder is distinguishing red and green (Brettel, Vienot & Mollon, 2004). Some shapes can, for men, flow into one another and thereby make it difficult to recognise the image. This perception also affects recognition of the Amstel brand, which is depicted among many other details.

Furthermore, the image contains a lot of atmosphere and amusing details but has no real action, hook or idea on which men can focus. Men clearly have more need for originality. To attract them, a surprising punch line or an amusing pun is needed (Van Putten, 2003). There is a high probability that men won't notice this ad because they cannot discern what the ad is trying to convey. A layout with lots of detail more quickly passes a perception threshold in men and is therefore less accessible to them. For men, a layout should be uncluttered and functional. Men scan a layout for the essentials and spend relatively shorter time on them (Meyers & Sternthal-Levy, 1991). An advertisement is sometimes compared to a two-second commercial. This short time period will, in this situation, probably be too short for men.

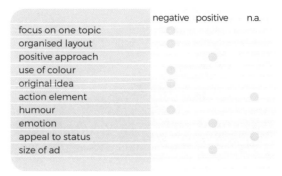

	negative	positive	n.a.
focus on one topic	●		
organised layout	●		
positive approach		●	
use of colour	●		
original idea	●		
action element			●
humour	●		
emotion		●	
appeal to status			●
size of ad		●	

134

AGENCY: PROMOTIONAL SOURCE, AMSTERDAM

BODY ADDICTION AD

This ad by Bartle Bogle Hegarty (BBH) London is particularly unclear for men because the image is too complex to discern. A layout aimed at men should be simple and focused on a single theme, which should preferably be captured in a single image, together with a short description that includes one or two features (Putrevu, 2001).

The ad refers to an 'appetising' man with the phrase, 'Feel good enough to eat'. The target audience, however, will not literally picture themselves in the man's position. The message is positive, but the ad's message is unclear. Does it have something to do with aftershave? The advertisement's positive qualities are its large and notable shape and its unusual delivery.

The use of colour is also confusing when combined with the underlying shape of a male model. The combined use of red and green is too extensive, which would result in perception problems for approximately 10% of men. Combined with the capricious shapes, the camouflaged image is extremely difficult for men to recognise. The man in the advertisement is hiding behind a tasty-looking fruit dessert. Men, however, identify more with factors such as boldness, heroism, problem solving and success, none of which are reflected in this advert. This man in the advert appears to be rather insecure and is almost completely disguised as a dessert. He is not a hunter or initiator but rather is passive in this situation, probably in anticipation of a potential lover who seeks a delicious prince instead of a tough, independent partner. It is unlikely that men would identify themselves in such a situation.

136

	negative	neutral	positive	n.a
focus on one topic	●			
organised layout	●			
positive approach			●	
use of colour	●			
original idea		●		
action element				●
humour		●		
emotion			●	
appeal to status	●			
size of ad			●	

AGENCY: BARTLE BOGLE HEGARTY, LONDON

9.2 ADS SUITABLE FOR MEN

MG SPORTS CAR AD

This advertisement consists of two successive spread ads. The ad is likely to score high on pre-attentive processing. In this phase, viewers react to words and images that are stored in our hippocampus (memory). This process is entirely physiologically determined and is monitored by the senses in the subconscious of our nervous system (Sille, 2005; Hulsebos, 2005).

What is immediately striking is that there is no one in the cell. The second spread immediately clarifies the situation. Fantasy and dream become a reality according to a very spectacular, incomparable escape, which is a sensation that every man dreams of.

This ad has all the ingredients of a great ad for men, such as the emotions of adventure, excitement and escape. The poster with the convertible sports car represents these values, while the heading expresses, 'The ultimate freedom'. In the first spread, the male viewer's focus is drawn to the poster on the prison wall. This view is very subtly directed because the ad is almost colourless. Colours are less important for men because they derive fewer useful emotions from them. Men think more in instrumental values (functional information), such as horsepower, number of cylinders and top speed (Capello, 2005).

Men on average are more agile and sporty and need more space (Alexander, 1986; Moir & Jessel, 1990). Solitary confinement is therefore a brutal punishment in which an individual loses control over the environment. The ad, however, provides an improbable solution: the undetected escape after which he is probably on his way ro a red MG sports car (men attach value to this idea) (Van Putten, 2003).

The size of the ad is ideal because the male viewer is completely focused on the image. The choice of a subject without any distracting body text or additional images is also a plus.

The ad is based on a positive end result. It reinforces the focus on solutions, skills and big ideas, all of which are psychological characteristics that men base their self-worth upon and that can be linked to the brand association of MG.

	neutral	positive
focus on one topic		●
organised layout		●
positive approach		●
use of colour	●	
original idea		●
action element		●
humour		●
emotion		●
appeal to status		●
size of ad		●

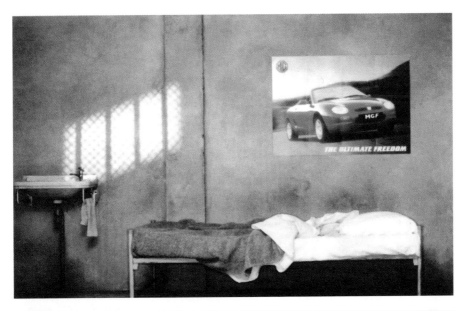

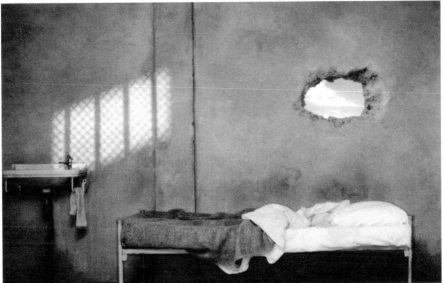

AGENCY: UBACHS WISBRUN, AMSTERDAM

DELTA LLOYD INSURANCE AD

To enjoy this advertisement one should perhaps, as a man, have below-average empathic abilities, implying that this ad is less suitable for women. The ad centres on four tough riot police, one of whom is a little person. All four are on horseback and in full riot gear. Despite this, the perception is that the little riot policeman is less able of coping with the task at hand. The background image emphasises the challenge of a special police unit's job.

Men tend to see just the humour in this image, without worrying about the little person's possible suffering. This image exemplifies courage, perseverance and a willingness to take significant risks, which seem to be completely shielded by the very loyal insurance company Delta Lloyd. In this ad, the company positions itself as the insurer of tough men, providing complete coverage for irresponsible and risky behaviour that might lead to injury. The ad uses a positive approach that is visualised in a humorous way, which appeals to the male brain. Men appreciate this unrealistic setting and allow their imaginations to run wild as to what could happen in such a situation. Men are also less sensitive to the social impact, which is something women would notice. The Delta Lloyd's message is clear and direct: 'We take good care of our policyholders'. Men want to be approached more directly, and their attitude often is, 'Be direct and to the point, with no detours and no complicated wording'. They will put in less effort if understanding something requires a detour (Wolff, 2005).

The text bar '... definitely Delta Lloyd' just below the (latent) victim almost literally underlines what Delta Lloyd stands for. The layout is simple and clearly focused on one topic. The use of colour is sober and functional. This is an ad that is probably meant for both sexes, but it clearly communicates better to men.

	neutral	positive
focus on one topic		●
organised layout		●
positive approach		●
use of colour		●
original idea		●
action element		●
humour		●
emotion		●
appeal to status	●	
size of ad		●

140

... zeker delta lloyd

AGENCY: TBWA/CAMPAIGN COMPANY, AMSTERDAM
'... certain delta lloyd.' (The Dutch word 'zeker' has two meanings: 'being secure' and 'being sure'.)

BAVARIA BEER AD

This ad illustrates why good advertisements for men do not need a human aspect. The message here could be considered simplistic. Give your father one or two crates of Bavaria beer for Father's Day and he will come up with at least nine ways to use them.

The idea is based on an extremely cognitive, linear thinking pattern from cause to effect (Van Putten, 2003; Capello 2005). The ad demonstrates that feelings and affection for design, the use of colour, application capability, harmony and empathy are not innate male talents. Some men from the core target group are perhaps even somewhat proud of this fact. This core group, on which Bavaria focuses, probably prefers to be associated with this cool attitude.

The ad implicitly shows that routing within the selection process in men is primarily provided by neuro-cognitive processes (the left brain) and to a lesser extent through the emotional right brain. Therefore, the ad communicates a high level of functionality. You can almost feel the partner's disapproval and resistance to her boyfriend or husband wanting to use a beer crate as a TV stand.

Due to their greater capacity for empathy, women are much more capable of assessing situations based on their emotional value. Thus, I think many women will understand this ad (and many other ads for men) and will feel vindicated in terms of their superior empathic abilities as compared with those of men. With men, these ideas work purely through humour, which works in a more complicated manner in women, who tend to have a broader perspective on a seemingly simple situation. Therefore, this humorous approach is more effective for men than for women.

	negative	positive	n.a.
focus on one topic		●	
organised layout		●	
positive approach		●	
use of colour		●	
original idea		●	
action element			●
humour		●	
emotion		●	
appeal to status	●		
size of ad		●	

De tips voor vaderdag.

Voetenbankje.

CD-rek.

Gereedschapskist.

TV-meubel.

Visstoeltje.

Werkbank.

Koelbox.

Bijzettafeltje.

Minibar.

Zo, nu eerst'n Bavaria

AGENCY: DMB & B WORLDWIDE COMMUNICATIONS, AMSTERDAM
'The tips for father's day. Footrest, CD rack, Toolbox, TV cabinet, Fishing chair, Workbench, Cooler, Coffee table, Minibar'

9.3 ADS UNSUITABLE FOR WOMEN

VALISÈRE LINGERIE AD

This ad for Valisère push-up bras contains a kind of humour that is not likely to appeal to women. In fact, one might suspect that this ad was developed by men. Men tend to be more outspoken between each other than women do. The topic of breasts has a different meaning among men. For women, the joke usually has a broader, deeper and more personal meaning. This ad likely oversteps the limits of decency for most women (Key, 2005; Capello, 2005).

Men have a narrower range of emotions, and therefore misclassify many 'misunderstood' emotions as humour. Typical examples include subtle but sad situations that require a reasonably developed sense of empathy. Women are better at analysing such situations and putting them into words. They therefore don't see those situations as humorous (Brunt, 2005).

Women will immediately notice that everyone in this advertisement is too close to each other and that the man directly behind the woman in question would likely make physical contact with her with the slightest movement. Women will see this as a form of sexual harassment, given that they appear to react extremely sensitively to pressure on the skin on almost every part of the body. This tactile sensitivity is significantly greater for children and women than for men. In certain trials, even the least sensitive woman had a better sense of touch than the most sensitive man (Moir & Jessel, 1990).

The row of people also looks a bit artificial, and there is little vibrancy in the image. They all seem to be standing at attention with their arms by their sides. Women tend to notice these non-verbal details much more quickly than men. However, responses to the clothing in this example are disregarded.

This image might also depict a woman being embarrassed by the wandering hands of the man in front, who, by looking closely, sees the desperation in the woman's feet. She recoils from the apparently unwanted advances of the man in front of her and is thus pushed towards the person behind her. It is evident that humour is much more complicated for women than it is for men.

The colour scheme of the image is a little gloomy for an ad aimed at women. A woman is first attracted to the big picture and must be able to identify with the image. In this image, she sees an insecure person of her sex who feels uncomfortable among all of these men. None of the men is really being gallant and keeping sufficient distance to preserve her privacy. The insecure woman is also being tormented by an uneasy and oversized push-up bra, which is probably not an effective humorous approach for women.

144

Push-up Bra · valisère · lingerie

AGENCY: DDB DM9, SÃO PAULO

	negative	positive	n.a.
overall atmosphere	●		
detailed information	●		
human element		●	
eliminates negative emotion	●		
eliminates sex or violence	●		
use of colour	●		
rich in details	●		
rich in emotion			●
nonverbal signs	●		
creates 'we' feeling	●		

OLAY ANTI-WRINKLE CREAM AD

This ad for Oil of Olay has a great concept with a complete conviction about what the product promises. Strategically speaking, the ad is strongly oriented towards a solution. I strongly suspect that a man made this ad since a quick solution to a problem is crucial to men.

Women don't always immediately start looking for the solution, but often want more information about what the product will do for them. Therefore the information in this ad is too limited.

Women are also susceptible to subjective communication, but this message contains a certain overpromise to really be convincing. Men are cognitive processors and will rapidly calculate the probability with as a result: when the promise isn't fulfilled, the actual result may also be good enough.

Women will appreciate the humour of the ad but at the same time have some aversion to the overall feel. This may also be due to the sober use of colour and the absence of informative captions. Having a human aspect in the ad is a positive, but the male model leaves a detached non-verbal impression.

Women are social creatures and are very sensitive to the general atmosphere in the social environment. If the exposure and the styling of the ad showed more warmth (more feeling and dedication), this ad would be more appealing to the female sex. Another improvement would be the male model winking and mischievously smiling at the camera.

It's a pity that good ideas don't always come across properly and are less effective because of it.

	negative	positive	n.a.
overall atmosphere	●		
detailed information	●		
human element		●	
eliminates negative emotion			●
eliminates sex or violence			●
use of colour	●		
rich in details	●		
rich in emotion		●	
nonverbal signs		●	
creates 'we' feeling	●		

146

AGENCY: SAATCHI & SAATCHI, DUBAI

9.4 ADS SUITABLE FOR WOMEN

BLICKER SHOES AD

This advertisement for the shoe brand Blicker symbolises, in a subtly strategic way, that 'the shoe' perhaps represents the most important garment for a woman. The ad is transparent, has a cosmetic look and exudes, as it were, femininity.

Many women like to picture themselves as princesses and want to maintain a girly appearance for as long as possible. The watercolour illustration shows subtle and flowing brushstrokes that strongly accentuate the female figure.

The creators understood what women prefer: long, slender legs; a narrow waist; long and voluminous hair; long, narrow fingers; and large, prominent eyes. A single dark brushstroke in the hair subtly shows a likely current trend. Women have a special eye for such details.

In the heading 'Schuhe, die anziehen', the word 'anziehen' has a double meaning. The heading's literal meaning is 'shoes that dress you'; however, the second meaning of anziehen is something along the lines of 'while increasing attractiveness and appeal'.

For the typography, a script font (from a handwritten letter) was chosen. Handwritten script has a human aspect that also appeals to women, who often search for interpersonal dialogue. The red dot at the end of the logo subtly refers to the visual in the shape of a

shoe. Women often look at the big picture (Van Putten, 2003). The right mood in an advertisement is very important to them, and just one misplaced detail or an unattractive ambience in an image can make an advertisement completely uninteresting. Therefore, the details in an advertisement for women are very important. Women immediately notice subtle nuances in the face, such as small colour changes. A woman's product selection process is largely based on details and ambience.

This advertisement shows that communication aimed at women can have many subtle details, but it need not be overly detailed or cluttered in order to be able to communicate effectively. A degree of calmness in a layout and a focus on a single subject communicate more clearly to both sexes. Fine nuances and nonverbal innuendos are effective elements for women.

	neutral	positive	n.a.
overall atmosphere		●	
detailed information	●		
human element		●	
eliminates negative emotion			●
eliminates sex or violence			●
use of colour		●	
rich in details		●	
rich in emotion		●	
nonverbal signs		●	
creates 'we' feeling		●	

Schuhe, die anziehen.

AGENCY: WEIGERTPIROUZWOLF, HAMBURG

'Shoes to attract' (play on words: the German 'anziehen' means 'attract' as well as 'dress' or in the case 'become you').

BEVERLY HILLS HOTEL AD

This ad succeeds because of the atmosphere conveyed by the images. Women need to be able to see themselves within an advertisement for it to be effective. Women focus more often on non-verbal cues in a layout and are more inclined to look for the symbolism within the image or the picture's atmosphere. Women are also more sensitive to the colour harmony and image information. They possess greater empathy and more often look for affinity, acceptance, admiration, idealism and dedication (Putrevu, 2001; Van Putten, 2003).

The copy in the ad is entirely in a script (handwritten) font, which often has interpersonal emotions hidden within. Women are better able to interpret these fine nuances in handwriting and the presence of possible emotional signals. In addition, women often orient themselves based on non-verbal cues within a layout. They are capable of receiving more signals and interpreting and articulating them in more variations. Due to their greater empathy, women can easily identify themselves with the target audience. Moreover, women often rely on their intuition (Van Putten, 2003; Capello, 2005).

Women probably find it more fun to follow advertisements than men (Wolff, 2005). The content of this text is based on a personal experience and is appealing because women consciously take part in a storyline and tend to experience the story from the inside. These ads are based on shopping experiences, personal feelings about the surroundings of Beverly Hills and probably spontaneous friendships (Moir & Jessel, 1990). In addition, the precise choice of words in the text is important because women have greater linguistic abilities and therefore find it easier to become involved in the storyline (Alexander, 1986; Putrevu, 2001). Texts such as these, based on social life, are also more effective for women because women devote more time to their social life than men do (Alexander, 1986).

The photography is entertaining, detailed, elegant, and subtle and it exhibits an appealing setting for women. The layout is playful because of the human touch in the script font, the slanted picture and the caption that reads, 'Love Beverly Hills, xx'. This layout suggests a relationship with the reader and is casual and naturally inviting to read. An interesting detail is that the eyes are not visible in either of the ads, which were likely hidden to keep the model anonymous so that the reader could identify herself with her.

Women embrace advertising that is verbally and visually rich and contains a complex vocabulary and detailed information. To women, advertising with subjective content and an image-oriented message has remarkable appeal. Women also appear to be more sensitive to non-verbal communication, more visually oriented and more romantic than men (Putrevu, 2001).

I know a ten thousand story hotel.

I'll show you a place where Charlie Chaplin was anything but silent, the bar the Rat Pack called their regular watering hole, and the pool where Raquel Welsh was discovered. Visit soon, we'll create a few stories of our own.
Love, Beverly Hills xx

Is it shopping or sightseeing? It's hard to tell.

I know a place with more views than the Eiffle Tower. It's more colorful than Rio, and has more dangerous curves than the Pyrenees. Visit soon, there's lots I'd like to show you.
Love, Beverly Hills xx

AGENCY: M&C SAATCHI, SYDNEY

	positive	n.a.
overall atmosphere	●	
detailed information	●	
human element	●	
eliminates negative emotion		●
eliminates sex or violence		●
use of colour	●	
rich in details	●	
rich in emotion	●	
nonverbal signs	●	
creates 'we' feeling	●	

CONTREX MINERAL WATER AD

This advertisement is very successful because there is a clear relationship between the shape of the plastic bottle and a woman's waist. Women typically spend more time on their appearance than men. An Australian study showed that girls as young as six were dissatisfied with their weight and appearance. The double-page ad is predominantly blue (The Independent, 2005). In contrast to other ads for women, the colour in this ad is used sparingly. This is not without reason, given that women prefer blue over red, while men prefer red. Women are also more sensitive to light from the low-frequency part of the spectrum and therefore see more shades of blue than men (Moir & Jessel, 1990). Women are also more susceptible to pastel shades and soft colour hues (Van Nunen, 2005; Wolff 2005). A subtle pink accent adorns the word mark and can also be found in the edges of the label. These kinds of colour combinations are quickly noticed by women. Pastel shades like these will not often be used for men because men are less able to perceive these colours (Van Nuenen, 2005).

The overall image symbolises the purity and beauty of the female body, while the embossed pattern in the bottle relates to ornate clothing. A Contrex bottle gives confidence because its water cleanses the body and ensures a lasting slim figure. It is the helping hand against looming obesity. After yielding to temptation, as it were, the water rinses away the sinful fat. Contrex can thus be seen as a beacon among temptations. A woman attaches much more importance to ideal beauty, while being aware that some body parts have clearly been manipulated by extensive retouching (Capello, 2005). The heading 'Mon partenaire minceur' loosely translates as 'My slim partner', which speaks of the relationship or trust with the Contrex brand. Women sense a lot more, collect material, relativise, think back and thus develop their choice. The consequence of this approach is that they doubt themselves much more frequently than men. Women are also more sensitive to atmosphere and search for more self confirmation. This approach can make a woman more insecure (Capello, 2005). The Contrex brand can help a woman overcome her insecurity and manifests itself as her partner, friend or companion who provides support in difficult times when discipline is required.

The subtle detail of a belly button piercing shows that an ornament looks better with a slender waist. The body is transparent, so everyone can both look at it and see through it. No more uncertainty; everything is pure, transparent and clear with the help of Contrex mineral water. The ad tells this with a minimal use of copy. Women are more inclined to look for the symbolism of the image or to discover the atmosphere of the picture. Women are also more sensitive to the harmony between the applied colour and the suggested information in the image (Putrevu, 2001; Van Putten, 2003; Van Nunen, 2005). The design of the ad is very dependent on taste. Women are more precise in the field of design and pay more attention to details. Design is also a form of visual communication and is generally more effective for both sexes than verbal communication (Van Nunen, 2005).

AGENCY: M&C SAATCHI, PARIS
'My partner in losing weight'

	negative	positive
overall atmosphere		●
detailed information	●	
human element		●
eliminates negative emotion		●
eliminates sex or violence		●
use of colour		●
rich in details		●
rich in emotion		●
nonverbal signs		●
creates 'we' feeling		●

9.5 ADS SUITABLE FOR MEN AND WOMEN

AUDI CAR BRAND AD

This double-page ad is successful for both men and women because it refers to two important values: The instrumental value of 115 horsepower (aimed at men) and the expressive value of a disappointed daughter, aimed at women.

The girl at the bottom of the stairs probably just saw and heard that her father is suddenly in the possession of a new Audi A4, while her wish for a horse goes ungranted. This is a very familiar situation (at least for anyone who has the budget to buy a similar car). It is clear that a man's product selection process is virtually independent of the environment and is based mainly on his own opinion. The girl is probably supported by her mother, who, in general, takes notice of her social environment. The daughter is likely to have been aware of the consideration to purchase an Audi and probably intercepted various bits of conversation between her parents. The mother likely mentioned other things that needed attention, such as her daughter's desire to own a horse. It's likely that during those discussions it soon became apparent that her father was less environment dependent and that he relied much more on his own opinion when making choices (Putrevu, 2001; Meyers-Levy & Sternthal, 1991; Hupfer, 2002). This ad succinctly illustrates men's and women's recurring dilemma in the product selection process. Of course, a woman loves luxury and comfort, but she takes her surroundings into account. The DDB agency almost certainly knows about this insoluble dilemma and plays with the tempting aspects of the selection process. For example, men make decisions based on the conditions, unlike women. How do they each come to a decision? There is the underlying thought of the budget to be taken into account. Do they opt for the Audi brand or a cheaper, lesser-known and less status-conscious brand? The ad actually gives the answer itself. Audi has positioned itself with a confident attitude and is apparently well aware of its brand position. The ad enters into a dialogue with both sexes, and this advertisement is more accessible for women because they are probably better able to follow the dialogue (Wolff, 2005).

The mother intuitively knows that her husband is most strongly influenced by a sense of status and is less led by social environmental factors (Key, 2005).

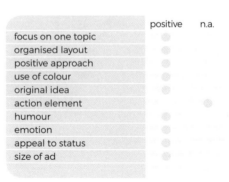

	negative	positive	n.a.
overall atmosphere		●	
detailed information	●		
human element		●	
eliminates negative emotion		●	
eliminates sex or violence			●
use of colour		●	
rich in details		●	
rich in emotion		●	
nonverbal signs		●	
creates 'we' feeling		●	

	positive	n.a.
focus on one topic	●	
organised layout	●	
positive approach	●	
use of colour	●	
original idea	●	
action element		●
humour	●	
emotion	●	
appeal to status	●	
size of ad	●	

AGENCY: DDB, BRUSSELS

Men are more independent, self-oriented and competition oriented (Putrevu, 2001). Her average higher emotional quotient makes her life less simple than that of the average man. She cannot easily choose between these two variables (a horse or a car) and will always take into account the social aspects as described here. According to Capello (2005) and Wolff (2005), women do more 'sensing', material collecting, relativising and recollecting.

The consequence of this approach is that they are much more often in doubt and more frequently look for affirmation of their choices. Men are not inhibited by such things. They go straight for the goal and show more self-confidence (Capello, 2005). Women have a greater empathy than men, which is not always seen as an advantage. The lack of empathy in men makes it easier for them to choose for themselves.

Women sometimes desire this independent way of thinking and might envy the uncomplicated way of men. In this case, there is the feeling of responsibility that the average (working) woman has for her family (Wolff, 2005).

The heading: 115 horses. Just for your father. This joke will have a very different meaning to both sexes, making it clear that humour has a different effect on men and women. Men see this as the joke, the idea of 115 horsepower versus one horse (probably just a pony). Women will understand the joke but will also take into account the social and environmental factors, immediately making the joke less funny. In addition, women equally strive for status, but it depends on the opinion of others. In this case, the girl will really come into possession of a pony!

MINOLTA PHOTO CAMERA AD

The billboard with the advertisement for the new waterproof photo camera from Minolta has two aspects that appeal to both men and women.
First, there is the social side. Women prefer a human message that talks to the viewer. Women have a wider view of the world in which human intuition plays a central role. Women are looking for a human brand (Key, 2005). This advertisement not only effectively shows the benefits of this small family camera but also refers to the fact that technique is subservient to man. Minolta touts its user friendliness, unlike many competitors who often focus too deeply on the technical details and thereby fail to communicate well with the female sex.

The peeing toddler evokes emotions in women such as sweetness, cuteness and pampering. Women want to identify with an advertisement. They seek symbolism with which to explore the atmosphere of the picture. They possess greater empathy and more frequently look for affinity, acceptance, admiration, idealism and commitment (Van Putten, 2003). She recognises the importance of a camera that can capture a drop of water and realises the possibilities and opportunities for capturing her surroundings. For women the social aspect is very important, which does not mean that there always has to be a 'human presence' in an advertisement but that a 'social dimension' is preferred (Alexander, 1986).

Men are much more fascinated with the original idea of a peeing poster and the technique behind it. To them, there is a certain feeling of competition; 'I wish I had thought of this; it's brilliant!' On the other hand, men also find this peeing toddler a bold and cool image. A boy who is barely two years old already has so much courage? Boys strongly identify themselves with such a toddler, giving their imagination free rein, such as, 'If I were that small, I would definitely do it that way!' Men adopt a more adventurous vocabulary and are generally more creative and inventive (Moir & Jessel, 1990). Their child-like fantasy world develops well into adulthood. 'In men, you more often suddenly see the boy' (Dresselhuis, as cited in Camps, 2001).

The male sphere of interest lies more in sports, action and movement (Alexander, 1986). Men clearly need more originality. A surprising punch line, a clever pun or a special music clip is needed to attract men. The link to the product or brand should remain well preserved, otherwise men's attention will quickly flag. However, this does not mean that women are not susceptible to original advertising. An advertisement with an original concept quickly attracts the attention of both sexes and scores higher in terms of brand image and brand awareness (Van Putten, 2003).

156

AGENCY: KKBR/SMS, AMSTERDAM

'The camera that can handle a splash'. (The Minolta photocamera is water resistent. 'Tegen een spatje kunnen' (Can handle a splash) is a pun on the Dutch saying 'tegen een een stootje kunnen', which means: can take a beating.)

	negative	positive
overall atmosphere		●
detailed information	●	●
human element		●
eliminates negative emotion		●
eliminates sex or violence		●
use of colour		●
rich in details		●
rich in emotion		●
nonverbal signs		●
creates 'we' feeling		●

	negative	positive
focus on one topic		●
organised layout		●
positive approach		●
use of colour		●
original idea		●
action element		●
humour		●
emotion		●
appeal to status	●	
size of ad		●

DIAMOND INFORMATION CENTRE AD

This spread ad performs well for both sexes because men are evaluated based on their deficient romantic and empathic abilities. The ad shows how love is enveloped in nuance. Each gift contains a form of symbolic value.

Women are pleasantly surprised by signs of affection that confirm a personal relationship. They are more sensitive to subtle nonverbal cues such as a smile and an elegant gesture. They seek the approval of others and appreciate positive verbal allusions. For example, women are relationship-oriented and enjoy being surprised by small (spontaneous) gifts that confirm their mutual friendship (Putrevu, 2001).

A man naturally uses a cognitive thought process and is less able to put his feelings into words (Moir & Jessel, 1990). The creators of this ad seem to know this and symbolically imply this in the ad by stating 'When you cannot put it into words, put into giving.'

Women naturally seem to have more feeling for aesthetic matters. Their sophisticated perception leads to more attention to details. Women can generally perceive colours more accurately and can better distinguish subtle colour nuances. Women have a better sense of proportion in terms of colour and structure. In addition, ads aimed at women can dare to experiment with more colours and shapes. Designs intended for women should be full of subtle details and emotions, both in colour and human aspects. Women are able to perceive and process many different details. Designs can also be very romantic and evoke emotions from the past, such as retro influences from films and the fashion world.

The kind of humour expressed in this ad is suitable for both sexes and will be interpreted by both in the same manner. In this example, the humour wherein men are subject to criticism will be more socially accepted (Brunt, 2005).

	negative	neutral	positive	n.a
overall atmosphere		●		
detailed information			●	
human element			●	
eliminates negative emotion			●	
eliminates sex or violence				●
use of colour	●			
rich in details			●	
rich in emotion			●	
nonverbal signs			●	
creates 'we' feeling			●	

	neutral	positive
focus on one topic		●
organised layout		●
positive approach		●
use of colour		●
original idea		●
action element	●	
humour		●
emotion		●
appeal to status		●
size of ad		●

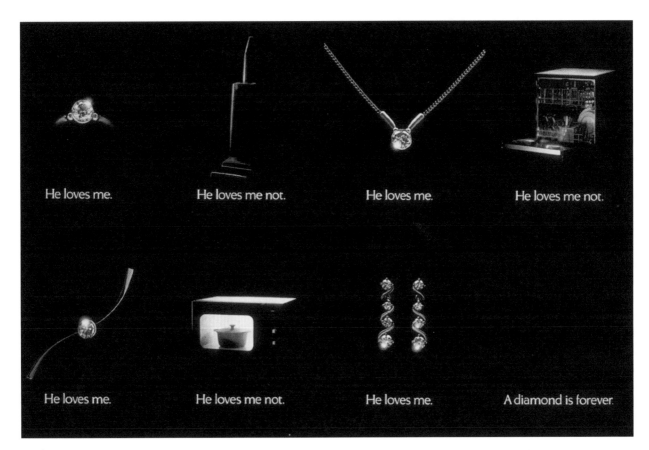

AGENCY: J. WALTER THOMPSON, LONDON

9.6 TEN BASIC RULES FOR CREATING EFFECTIVE ADVERTISING FOR WOMEN

1. Ensure that the entire print image contains the right atmosphere. Women are sensitive and will lose interest if the atmosphere is inadequate. Pay attention to details, because women will notice imperfections and artificial details quickly.

2. Improve the ambience by adding small images or short messages. Women prefer elaborate and detailed information such as analogue communication (non-verbal communication), where smell, taste, visual, aural and tactile details are incorporated.

3. Make sure a social or human element is incorporated into the expression. Women respond less when there is an explicit emphasis on the product or brand itself. They will show less interest in technical issues or an explanation of those issues. Women will, however, show interest when told what a product or service can provide them.

4. Include factors that interest women and remove factors that are unappreciated. Both negative and positive emotions are effective on women.

5. Be consistent and precise in your choice of words. Provide encouragement and avoid topics that have any relation to sex. Explain associations from a personal experience and incorporate an appropriate story.

6. Incorporate emotional elements such as sensitivity or vulnerability into your copy platform. Women enjoy sharing feelings with the people they trust. Many of these feelings take place in a rational atmosphere, where brands can play also a role.

7. Experiment with colour and/or create expressions that are colourful. Where necessary, use nuanced colour. Women possess a superior sensory ability that allows them to perceive stimuli better and more intensely.

8. Spend time into your typography by using extra space between letters or interlines, fine details, nuances in colour, subtle fonts, handwritten writing or script. Women are detailed processors and will there focus more on typographical details.

9. Make use of non-verbal signs and subjective, image-oriented clues. Women possess the ability to empathise and will therefore notice subtle non-verbal details and small signs of mimicry more easily.

10. Make sure to appeal to a 'collective feeling'. Women look for a connection within a group and are more loyal to the people within a company than to the company itself.

9.7 TEN BASIC RULES FOR CREATING EFFECTIVE ADVERTISING FOR MEN

1. Make sure that the advertisement is focused on a single subject. Men are less capable of spreading their attention over multiple factors or details. A beautiful female model distracts a man from the essence of an advertisement.

2. Base your advertisement on an original idea or an unorthodox setting. Men like to be surprised by striking details and can greatly appreciate surprising clues.

3. Concentrate on the product or brand; a human presence is not necessary. Men react effectively to objects and to people.

4. Whenever possible, add an element of action and incorporate some sort of challenge within your image or copy content. Men are competitive and value action.

5. Ensure your information mentions practical facts including horsepower (HP), pixels, clock rate, and clutch power or include technical imagery, maps, bar graphs or general graphics. Men are cognitive processors and react effectively to data.

6. Stay formal and convey your story clearly, without taking unnecessary detours. Men are less capable of following a story and often focus on the essence. They tend to separate side details from the essence more quickly than women.

7. Approach a man positively and add humour where necessary. Humour is very effective on men. Men receive more energy from a positive approach.

8. Ensure you approach the individual and appeal to their personal status, power, knowledge, craftsmanship and aspects that will impress others.

9. Use bright primary colours along with actions or choose only monotone colours. Try to avoid nuances in colours given the significant rate of colour vision disorders in men.

10. Do not focus too much on human emotions or emotions in general. Men have a narrower emotional spectrum and will lose interest if there is too much focus on emotions.

10.CONCLUSIONS

The findings of this book are further interpreted in this chapter. The concept of conation

will be dissected and extensively discussed. KPIs are defined which ultimately leads to a new

mathematical model. The results provide insight about where a person is located on the scale

of masculinity/femininity. Knowing this is essential for well-targeted neuro advertising.

However, I would already be amazed if I could make a small contribution to unravel

the mystery of man versus woman.

$$++/+ \; + \; ++/o \; = \; \textbf{FCA}$$

$$++/- \; + \; ++/+^2 \; = \; \textbf{MCA}$$

10.1 SEX DIFFERENCES IN NEUROBIOLOGY

There are significant neurobiological differences between men and women. Remarkably, the embryonic structure of both male and female brains starts out as female. However, if testosterone (the male hormone produced by the Y chromosome) interferes with the development, a baby's brain will be born with a male structure. This change does not happen instantly but rather in phases. The presence of either too much or too little testosterone results in an embryonic brain that does not fully develop into a male or female brain pattern. These fluctuations occur significantly less often during a female baby's development than that of a male baby. There are also considerably fewer mental and physical abnormalities with women later on in life. This fact leads to interesting data that imply that less extreme variations are expected with women than men in terms of behaviour.

10.2 COGNITIVE AND AFFECTIVE PROCESSES

THE SYMMETRICAL BRAIN

Female brains connect both cognitive and affective processes via a refined and detailed processor. This thought process is based on a symmetrical brain structure in which balance is achieved by a broader and fuller corpus callosum than in male brains. This broader and fuller corpus callosum ensures that there are more brain connections, so that a greater transfer of information between the two hemispheres is possible. Women consider various options, examine the possibilities and evaluate the possible consequences of their decision(s) more often than men. Women perceive important details and, as a result, often need more time than men to come to a well-grounded opinion. Women usually see more than one way to move forward and more often see a broad, horizontal and structured real-life perspective. This approach means that they experience everything in a broader manner, in which they value social relationships immensely. Women are generally more capable of handling the multiple aspects of a situation than are men. Women make no distinction between social and work-related issues and hence more easily find a balance between work and family. Such an elaborate process and consideration of cognitive and affective information can be seen as more successful and generally leads to effective evaluation and judgement.

This approach is also a form of long-term thinking in which women base their judgement on intuition, which is a subconscious thought process that cannot be rationalised. In short, women are superiour in making deliberate decisions that contain a social aspect.

AFFECTION

It is significant that women are more intrinsically affectionate than their male counterparts. This advantage is further reinforced by emotion spreading diffusely in both hemispheres of the female brain, in contrast to the male brain. There is therefore a greater chance for interaction with the limbic system, where the arousal of emotion is noted and sent to the neocortex for evaluation. These neurological qualities lead to feminine intuition. The left hemisphere of a female brain is better developed than the right hemisphere and has greater contact with the linguistic areas, which results in easier expression of both internal and extern stimuli.

THE AUTONOMOUS BRAIN

Male brains are dominated by either a cognitive or an affective thinking process, due to the reduced potential for information transfer between the hemispheres when compared with female brains.

The male brain has more specialised and limited functions and therefore has more difficulty spreading the attention among the left and right brain hemispheres. The male brain also finds it harder to switch between the two hemispheres.

However, the male brain's specialisation has the advantage of more easily focusing on a single subject without being distracted by emotional or cognitive considerations.

This converging concentration can lead men to become highly focused on a single issue. Numerous works of art and inventions are the direct result of these neurological specialties. However, many of these inventions were typically based on cognitive processes of a technical origin. In the male brain, the right hemisphere is larger than the left hemisphere, in contrast to the female brain. The right hemisphere represents visual, spatial and emotional qualities and is both specialised and limited, so that it can function more effectively.

COGNITION AND AFFECTION VERSUS TESTOSTERONE

The structure of the male brain during the embryonic development phase is determined by testosterone. Testosterone, an anabolic steroid, causes an increase in specific characteristics such as aggressiveness, competitiveness, self-assertion, self-assurance, independence, self-sufficiency, individualism and a reduced desire for comfort. The female sex also produces testosterone but in much smaller amounts. Male blood generally contains 20 times more testosterone than women's blood. Testosterone likely has a significant influence on male behaviour.

AFFECTION FOR COGNITION

Men have an effective but limited emotional spectrum. It is often said that men are better able to control their emotions; however, this could also be seen as a lack of emotional capability. Men have more trouble expressing their emotions but are capable of directing their emotions towards people and objects. This ability might explain the fact that men do not necessarily need the presence of a human in an advertisement for it to be effective.

THE COGNITIVE DOMINATE BRAIN

Men are considered as cognitive processors because they often think in a linear manner and make decisions based on selected, salient factors. Men also tend to disregard unimportant stimuli to achieve a certain goal as quickly and efficiently as possible. The male thinking process is channeled and emphasises the immediate problem rather than the context; the 'here and now' plays a key role for men. Men also tend to overestimate their abilities, which leads them to ignore details or take greater risks. The male consideration process is less meticulous, which is why they overlook small risks faster. Risk taking while ignoring details can be categorised as a form of short-term thinking that seeks quick results.

In conclusion, the male thought strategy is often based on the consideration of reasonably facts and perceived visible results. Men aim straight for the goal, step by step, through a cause-effect process, and frequently employ short-term strategies.

10.3 CONATION

FEMININE CONATIVE ATTITUDE

Women possess a symmetrical brain in which affection is inseparable from cognition. Women will therefore recognise a problem sooner but will have more trouble solving it, because the strong emotional component can interfere with finding (one-sided) solutions. Emotion is diffusely spread over both hemispheres. Cognition is located only in the left brain, which leads us to conclude that the emotional component is dominant in the female brain. Women are therefore likely to be more sensitive to their surroundings and more socially involved than are men.

MASCULINE CONATIVE ATTITUDE

Men often know how to separate affection from cognition, which leads them to more slowly recognise social issues but arrive at a (sometimes one-sided) solution more quickly. Cognition sometimes surpasses affection and vice versa with men. While the affective component is limited neurologically, which makes it function more effectively, the emotional spectrum is considerably smaller. With men, emotion is located only in the right brain, which is why men have a more dominant cognitive thinking process.

CONATION, THE RELATIONSHIP BETWEEN COGNITION AND AFFECTION

Conation depends on perception, and perception influences the behaviour or the behavioural intention. Behaviour intention or conation is dependent on two components: affection and cognition. When the affective component is dominant, the state is known as a feminine conative attitude. When the cognitive component is dominant, the state is known as a masculine conative attitude. If we take the value of affection and cognition into account, the result looks something like this:

AFFECTION		**COGNITION**		**CONATION**	
FEELING		**KNOWLEDGE**		**BEHAVIOUR**	

- Positive, negative or ambivalente feelings
- Motivation
- Creative
- Social

- Analyse
- Calculate
- Focus on solving
- Serial, linear

- Believe
- Hope
- Behavioural intention
- Engrossment

AFFECTION + COGNITION = CONATION

FEMININE CONATIVE ATTITUDE (FCA)		
AFFECTION + COGNITION = CONATION		
component ++/+	component ++/0	FCA

MASCULINE CONATIVE ATTITUDE (MCA)		
AFFECTION + COGNITION = CONATION		
component ++/-	component ++/+^{2}	MCA

Added value co-efficient/ talent factor: ++ = very good, +^{2} = good to very good, + = good, 0 = neutral, - = negative

AFFECTIVE OR COGNITIVE DOMINANCE

Affective dominance often expresses itself in specific characteristics or attitudes. Affection is a feeling that is often not directly externally portrayed by men or women (mostly in women) and is, therefore, less noticeable and often portrayed internally, and thus implicit.

Cognitive dominance is a thinking process that follows a serial and linear connection that results in a solution (mostly in men). Cognition is therefore quicker, more noticeable and externally focused, and thus explicit.

AFFECTIVE DOMINANCE
=
SCARCELY RECOGNISABLE
=
IMPLICIT

COGNITIVE DOMINANCE
=
CLEARLY RECOGNISABLE
=
EXPLICIT

IMPLICIT	EXPLICIT
Declarend	Doer
Caring	Protecting
Taking part in	Control
Indirect aggression	Direct aggression
Social well-being	Material well-being
Knight	Castle
Atmosphere	Matter
Internally	Externally
EQ	IQ
Breathing in	Breathing out
Ability	Power
Immaterial	Material

IMPLICIT	EXPLICIT
Smiling	Roaring with laughter
Atmosphere focused	Skill-focused
Status quo	Growth
Blue	Red
Pink	Light blue
Emphasis on mimicry	Emphasis on movement
Searching	Guiding
Sensitive	Formal
Divergent	Convergent
Spontaneous	Direct
Yang	Yin
Detail	Total

THE COGNITIVE PROCESS VERSUS CULTURE AND HEREDITY

A conative attitude can also be influenced by culture and heredity. When a particular culture promotes male values, it fosters and strengthens these values, increasing the masculine nature of an already masculine society while simultaneously suppressing feminine values. The Netherlands, for example, is a feminine society, which explains its social equality and complex (multi-tasking) communication processes.

Hereditary factors and environmental factors influence the degree to which a male embryo will fully develop as a male or female. Every male embryo starts out with a feminine brain that is transformed to the physical and mental gender of a male through the involvement of testosterone. During this transformation of the brain from feminine to masculine, certain errors may occur in different phases, which leads to an incomplete development of the male brain. In other words, there are probably more variants of male brains than there are of female brains in current society. When we add the components of culture and heredity to the formula, the result looks like this:

FEMININE CONATIVE ATTITUDE

Affection + Cognition + Culture + Heredity = Conation FCA
$++/+$ $++/0$ $+/-$ $+/++$

MASCULINE CONATIVE ATTITUDE

Affection + Cognition + Culture + Heredity = Conation MCA
$+/-$ $++/+^2$ $+/+$ $+/-$

10.4 GENDER DIFFERENCES IN PERCEPTION TOWARDS ADVERTISING

MEN ARE MORE INDIVIDUALISTIC

A man puts himself at the centre and often makes his decisions independently from his environment. A brand should approach a man as an individualist in order to form a bond. Persuasive communication is more effective with men when it refers to personal status, power, knowledge, craftsmanship and aspects that will impress others.

Men usually have a hierarchical mindset, finding their place within the correct rank, and will (where possible) attempt to move up the ladder. Men prefer to see these same values reflected in 'their brand'. Men reach satisfaction mostly from self-assertion and competitive behaviour, which has either a solution or accomplishment as a result.

The previously mentioned individualistic characteristics are not literally applicable, which is why we should keep in mind the following nuances. For example, one type of man will purposely avoid obtrusive behaviour, while another type might be less limited in his behaviour, taking advantage of all forms of power and showing off his accomplishments. A brand can respond to the developing tastes of its target audience by communicating more or less implicitly or explicitly.

HUMOUR

The male emotional spectrum is limited, that's why it works more effectively but on the other hand posses a more limited spectrum. Whereby only emotions are effective on men. This results in a more developed sense of humour. Persuasive communication based on humour works more efficient and effectively on the male psyche, because men are by nature more interested in positive stimuli.

For this reason, it is possible to use absurdity in the communication to form a bond with a brand. Men prefer thought patterns and dialogues with a surprising clue. Lateral thought patterns stimulate constructive thinking, and men are cognitive processors who tend to think step by step. However, when a step in the process is missed or is absolutely illogical, hilarity can ensue. The male sense of humour is reinforced by a natural absence of the ability to empathise, which leads men to categorise situations as humorous more often than women do.

WOMEN ARE INTRINSICALLY SOCIALLY INVOLVED AND SENSITIVE TO AMBIENCE

Women care a great deal for complete atmosphere and appearances in advertising and have a better eye for image details, which helps them notice artificial settings more easily. For example, imagine a bedroom where a woman is sleeping. The man perceives himself as part of that bedroom. A woman will notice more quickly whether the female model's makeup is properly applied or not. Women are also more capable of recognising human emotions during conversation, noticing more details when looking at advertising and forming an opinion regarding the atmosphere.

WOMEN ARE INTERESTED IN OTHER PEOPLE

Women are generally sensitive and are willing to make themselves vulnerable or dependent. A brand with particularly sensitive qualities will form a stronger bond with its female audience, which will help create a long-term relationship. Women therefore appreciate a brand that shows both its strong and weak points, which is why women, in general, prefer brands that are have more human aspects.

WOMEN ARE RELATIONAL PROCESSORS

Women are usually more romantic; one might say they possess certain antennae that allow them to experience sensitivity and vulnerability, and they expect these same impulses from the brand. Communication with a woman should focus on relationships, community and trust. A woman is a relational processor and is often more introverted. She will often look for the dialogue within advertising to better understand the message. This approach applies not only to films or novels but also to a single image that hides a bigger story. Iconic symbols with social components, such as deer, babies and young children, will reinforce the strong bond formed with the brand. Campaigns that conduct follow-ups on testimonials and open-ended advertising will be more effective because they trigger the romantic aspect of the relational process.

BROADER SPECTRUM OF EMOTIONS

Persuasive communication for women is most effective when it is based on human emotion. Women in general have a broader spectrum of emotions and, as a result, are more open. This openness leads to more effective cues for nearly all senses within the limbic system. Conative processes are, for the most part, controlled by emotion, which is why affective communication is more effective for women.

10.5 MEN/WOMEN FIT ADVERTISING

A significant difference between men and women is the fact that women have the ability to link cognition and affection during the thought process. Men either have a cognitive-dominated or affective-dominated thought process.

The female thought process includes a greater ability to empathise than men, which allows women to follow the male thought process (which usually is logical) more often and more easily. This ability would indicate that woman are capable of empathising with male emotions and that advertisements containing more male than female preferences would still communicate with both genders.

If the woman's ability to empathise is highly developed, she might be able to fully put herself into a man's shoes in certain cases. A female ninja who fights evil would be a fitting example, as women want to come off as strong. Women who take on the role of men in certain situations are acceptable to both genders. In some cases, it might even impress and attract men. However, this cross-gender role taking does not work the other way around, and often leads to amusing situations. Thus, the female component has the ability to make the communication acceptable for both genders in both directions. On one hand, she understands the male psyche better, while on the other she has the ability to take on a male role.

10.6 DIFFERENCES IN SENSES AND PERCEPTION

SUPERIOR FEMALE PERCEPTION

The symmetrical female brain appears to have greater contact with the limbic system, which enables women to experience a broader spectrum of emotions when compared with men, which in turn helps them perceive a greater range of emotions. Men react more effectively towards positive emotions and are therefore more specialised in positive emotions. According to theoretical and practical research, there is significant evidence that women excel in both positive and negative emotions. Thus we can conclude that positive and negative emotions that incorporate persuasive communication are as equally effective with women as they are with men.

Almost all stimuli (except olfactory) enter the brain via the thalamus, where the stimuli travel to specific brain areas such as the amygdala, also known as the emotional memory area. The amygdala has a more sophisticated link with all parts of the cerebral cortex or the associated cortex in women. We can conclude that women can experience stimuli in more detail and more intensely than men and that their senses are sharper than those of men.

THE MALE PERCEPTION

Men's spatial and visual abilities are more limited and more efficiently organised in the right brain.

This organisation makes the process of solving abstract problems a task performed only by the right brain. Visual and spatial abilities are better developed in men than in women, making it easier for men to read maps and manipulating 3-dimensional objects in their minds. Men's spatial cognitive ability is also more developed, which results in a better sense of coordination and more insight into spatial measures.

Even though their spatial and visual abilities are better developed, men's senses are more limited and less capable of handling stimuli. This is why men often want non-verbal stimuli to be visually compensated by images, maps, graphics, music or sound effects.

COLOUR SENSITIVITY

In comparison to men, women have superior colour perception. The female retina contains more cone cells, which help women perceive a greater number of colours. Women see more colour nuances and can differentiate them better, such as within the colour spectrum of red and blue. The broader emotional spectrum also plays a role in this perception. Women, in addition to possessing more cone cells than men, can perceive and identify individual colours more intensely, which probably has a significant influence on arousal. Women also perceive harmonic colours better, and their use of colour is often more flexible and diverse, which is why women often tend to experiment with colour.

Women also have more light-sensitive cones, which help them perceive more light impulses over a broader area. This greater number of light-sensitive and colour-sensitive cones helps women perceive colour in low-light conditions.

In general, men have lower colour sensitivity. One of every 12 men has a colour vision deficiency, most of whom have a problem with red and green. The percentage of women with this deficiency is significantly smaller. Only 1 of every 200 women has a colour vision deficiency. Even when there is absolutely no red/green colour deficiency, men often choose red over blue. With women, this preference is the other way around. Men's limited perception of colour probably explains why men usually care more for chromatic (saturation) colours or clear black-and-white contrasts. Out of all the pure colours, men mostly prefer cool grey over warm grey.

THE FORMAT OF AN ADVERTISEMENT

With men, the recognition and perception of an advertisement is very dependent on its placement within a medium. A small advertisement is more noticeable within a monotone background, as for example a classified advertisement on a contributing editor's website. Men in general do not like advertisements that contain too much information, because it can become confusing when combined with other advertisements. The size of an advertisement has a greater influence on men than on women. Most of the time, men will perceive a large advertisement as something dominant and will therefore consider it powerful.

With women, the above qualities do matter; however, women can give even more meaning to different sizes of advertisements. Women have more varieties to which they give meaning; for example, round, oval and complex shapes. While a man might link an aberrant shape to its meaning, a woman would not. Women often judge an advertisement on its subjective motives such as the use of colour, typography or perhaps even the atmosphere or setting. Women are usually less distracted by variations in an advertisement's shape.

TYPOGRAPHY

Women are capable of focusing on the information and even the atmosphere a font can deliver in terms of emotion. Women quickly perceive small nuanced differences in the use of a font, such as light versus ultralight fonts or normal, heavy, partly bold or bold fonts. In addition, small differences in font size or the use of a spatial interline can emphasise certain parts of the text. Letters can even be imbued with subtle colours or colour nuances to place extra emphasis on a certain emotion. Women can probably connect different meanings to a large number of available fonts. There are many possible ways to use typography to suit the atmosphere in advertising aimed at women.

Men are less able to divide their attention over multiple nuances. Men have trouble recognising differences in the use of a font. They become seduced by the style that reinforces the advertising target. However eventually, they too will focus on the content of the text itself. The use of clear contrasts to wempower the content is effective with men. Men require a very clear explanation as to the use of a font, given that they focus more on the originality of a font than on the use of the font. To men, a font can express action, dominance or movement. Men have a better-developed spatial ability and can comprehend and connect spatial shapes to layouts or moving images faster and more precisely than women. An excess of typographical elements within a layout will be more distracting for men than for women.

AGENCY: VOSCH THE BRAND GUIDE, OISTERWIJK
This is an example of a combination of
male and female typography.

LE GRAND LIT

COMPLEXITY OF A LAYOUT

In contrast to women, men are less capable of directing their attention over multiple activities.
Therefore, men often seem to focus only on the essence and ignore all other minor details, unlike women.

In order to process a message within a (complex) layout, we must access the information and motivation.
Access to the information is determined by the availability of a key or by cognition. The motivation
to convey a message (for example, within a layout) is driven by emotion. In other words:

- EMOTION IS THE MOTIVATION'S 'FUEL'.
- COGNITION IS 'THE KEY' TO A SOURCE OF INFORMATION.

Men probably possess a different form of emotion, the so-called 'converting emotion'. The male emotion
usually covers lower latitude results as opposed to the feminine emotion. On the other hand, the female
emotion is probably based on a diverging emotion. The female emotion often achieves higher results.
In other words, the female emotion covers a broad spectrum while the male is only pointed towards one
direction. This is the reason why men tend to focus on a specific subject, while women tend to focus on
multiple subjects/details simultaneously. Therefore, the male (converting) emotion prefers to focus its entire
motivation (emotion) on a single source of information (homocognition), while the female (diverging)
emotion is motivated to focus on multiple subjects or sources of information (heterocognition).

Female behaviour is
based on a diverging
emotion focused on
decentralised
(adherent) cognition.

Male behaviour is
based on a converging
emotion focused on
central (coherent)
cognition.

Adolescent Boy or girl from approximately 15 to 20 years of age.

Adolescence The transitional period between puberty and adulthood, in which the young person needs to develop his or her own identity. Syn. nubile (sexually mature).

Affective brain The right brain hemisphere, which spontaneously, directly, and intuitively reacts to observed stimuli. Emotional (affective or psychosocial) versus cognitive (knowledge). High versus low engagement.

Amygdala Greek for almond, is shown to be mostly connected to emotional reactions. The amygdala is also considered a 'guard' that carefully analyses every incoming signal and judges its emotional significance.

Anabolic Protein synthesis Improving the build-up of proteins and muscles.

Androgen Formed by andro (male) and gen (that which produces), a term for male sex hormones. Androgen hormones lead to male development forms.

Androgyne Someone of ambiguous sexual identity; one that combines major aspects of both the male and the female.

Androgyny Having both masculine and feminine characteristics. Greek meaning: man woman.

Anthropology Formed from the Greek ánthrōpos (human) + lógos (study). Study of man as a natural, historical being.

Arousal To stir to action.

Auditory ability Hearing.

Basal ganglia A group of brain structures around the thalamus that are engaged in the control of movement. See also Cerebellum.

Blind spot Area at the attachment of the optic nerve that is insensitive to light.

Brain See evolution of the brain.

Brain physiology Study of the function of the living brain. See also Physiology.

Brainstem The brainstem is important to vital functions such as body temperature, heart rate, respiration, and blood pressure. The brainstem is also essential in maintaining a sleep pattern, crying, urinating, chewing and changing pupil size.

Caudate nucleus The caudate nucleus or 'tail core' (Latin: cauda = tail; nucleus = core [4]) is a nucleus in the brain of many animal species. Initially, it was thought that this core, which forms part of the basal ganglia portion, was involved in the regulation of random motor skills. However, the caudate nucleus is an important component in learning and remembering, in particular when processing feedback. Both brain hemispheres have a caudate nucleus. They are located in the center of the brain, to the side of the lateral ventricle, and sit astride the thalamus. The core has a large head that becomes thinner and ends in a kind of tail.

Cell body or soma The spherical part of the neuron that contains the nucleus.

Cerebrum Largest part of the brain. Endbrain or telencephalon.

Cerebellum The cerebellum ensures fine tuning between perception and movement. Coordinates and regulates muscle activity. Images of newly learned movements are supposedly stored in the cerebellum.

Cingulate cortex A brain structure involved in the processing of pain stimuli, among other things. The cingulate cortex helps to process emotions and learning, plays a role in processing positive and negative reinforcement, such as a reward and punishment.

Cognitive brain The left brain hemisphere, which knows, analyses, thinks, calculates, considers, and decides.

Cognitive strategy, preferred The preferred use of a linear, cognitive thinking process.

Conative effects Effects related to will and behaviour, striving and wanting.

Conditioning (or being conditioned). Being predisposed to certain reactions, behaviour, opinions, etc., because of certain factors or circumstances.

Cones Located on the retina of the eye and responsible for the perception of colour. The cones are divided into 3 groups: red, green, and blue. The ratio is approximately 60% red, 30% green and 10% blue. Most of the cones are located at the outer edge of the retina. Our eye contains approximately 7 million cones. Chromatic subsystem.

Colour disorder Colour-blindness. A malfunction in the perception of colour. The most common colour disorder is the perception of the colours red and green. Approximately 1 in 12 Dutch men (8.3%) have a colour disorder. In Dutch women, this is 1 in 200 (0.5%). Men are more likely to be colour blind because the gene responsible for inherited colour blindness is passed on by the X-chromosome. Total colour blindness occurs in approximately 1 in 33,000 people. They see the world in black/white and shades of grey.

Colour disorders

Anomalous trichromacy	men	women
1. Protanomaly, red malfunction	1%	0.02%
2. Deuteranomaly, green malfunction	4.9%	0.38%
3. Tritanomaly blue malfunction	0.001%	0.001%
Dichromacy		
4. Protanopia, red defect	1.1%	0.01%
5. Deuteranopia, green defect	1.5%	0.002%
6. Tritanopia, blue defect	0.0025%	0.0025%

7. Monochromatic no cones, no colour (0.0001%)

The total failure to see colour is called achromatopsia.

Consciousness A state of being awake and aware of one's surroundings. Consciousness is primarily experienced through the prefrontal cortex.

Corpus A body or organ.

Corpus callosum A large mass of fibers between the left and right brain hemisphere. These nerve fibers enable the exchange of information between the two hemispheres. In women, the corpus callosum appears to be thicker and rounder than in men. The brain hemispheres connected by the corpus callosum have a larger number interconnections in women.

Corpus striatum Also called the striatum (or striped body), the corpus striatum is an area in the cerebrum beneath the cerebral cortex (cortex cerebri). The corpus striatum is an important part of the basal ganglia and controls the strengthening, inhibition, or adjustment of motor activity initiated by the cerebral cortex.

Cortex Outer layer of an organ.

Cortisol A corticosteroid. Cortisol is a hormone made from cholesterol in the adrenal cortex (see also Stress). It is sometimes called the stress hormone because it is released when any form of stress occurs, both physically and psychologically. It ensures certain proteins in muscles are broken down to release glucose (energy). Stress releases adrenaline and noradrenaline to make the body more alert and ready for fight or flight. Cortisol ensures compensation of this loss of energy.

Cues A cue is a stimulus that causes a change in the nervous system. A distinction can be made between external and internal stimuli. Examples of external stimuli are a lion, a bang, a kiss, a smell, and a brand. Examples of internal stimuli are memories of situations and experiences, such as engagement, sauna, eating ice cream, and experience with a brand.

Determinant A hereditary factor that dictates the development of a cell, an organ or somatic determinants for psychological life.

Deuteros Greek for second, indicating the colour green.

Dichromacy When the eye cannot perceive one of the colours. Red/green colour-blindness.

Dopamine A natural drug that plays a major role in love. The right amount of dopamine provides energy, feelings of joy, sharp concentration and a high amount of motivation to achieve rewards and pleasure.

Emotion Movere = Latin for 'moving'; 'e' means 'out'; an emotion literally means 'move out'.

Endocrine An internal secretion that is immediately absorbed into the bloodstream, such as from endocrine glands.

Endorphin A natural drug that creates a nice invigorating feeling. When our body gets tired from exercise, it will release endorphins because it thinks it is in danger and must keep moving. Endorphins provide extra energy, numb pain, and make the mind more alert. Also called the happiness hormone.

Engram Neural tissue in which memory is encoded.

Epiphysis cerebri See Pineal gland.

Estrogen Collective term for female sex hormones.

Evolution of the brain

Protoreptilian brain This part monitors the primary physiological needs such as: drinking, eating, sleeping, waking, blood pressure, body temperature, stool, and regulation of muscle tension. The primary function is to achieve and maintain an ideal balance. Processes that run automatically (500 million years) (Franzen & Bouwman, 1999).

Old cortex The frontal lobe and the limbic system. The term limbic system was introduced by Maclean (1952). He connected it to the evolution from the reptilian brain to the mammalian brain. The second oldest of the three parts of the brain, the limbic system, originated 200 million years ago. This section predominantly houses the emotions, the feelings, the short term memory (hippocampus) and the expressive reactions that are important for our self-preservation, such as joy, anger, fear, sadness, excitement, and boredom. We share this part with other mammals. The old cortex is responsible for habitual motivations such as the desire of women to care and the desire of men to protect, organize, fight, and dominate. The limbic system is very sensitive to images and analog communication, such as observations of postures, facial expressions, smells, and sounds (Franzen & Bouwman, 1999). Critical components are the amygdala, the cingulate cortex, and the hippocampus. The limbic system works in close collaboration with the hypothalamus, and some sections of the hypothalamus are also considered part of the limbic system (Het brein van A tot Z, 2003).

Neocortex The youngest and largest part of the brain, originating 50,000 years ago. Contains 20% of all brain (cerebral cortex) cells. It is the centerpiece of the higher brain functions such as speaking and understanding language, thinking, reading, writing, mathematics, analysis, music, ethics, morality, and other specific human characteristics. The cerebral cortex is divided into four lobes: the frontal, parietal, temporal, and occipital lobe.

Excitation Stimulation, incentive, a state of excitement.

Fovea A small pit in the retina filled with cones (no rods). This allows us to distinguish colour better and to focus. Responsible for sharp, central vision.

Frigidity Sexual insensitivity in women; disorder or condition in which no orgasm occurs during sexual intercourse.

Frontoparietal network The frontal and parietal lobe work together in complex cognitive functions, including memory, working memory, and attention. Together they form the frontoparietal network. The parietal lobe is fully grown around adolescence. The connections in the frontal lobe, however, continue to develop until the age of 30. After that time, this lobe will deteriorate.

Gender All social and cultural characteristics of one sex.

Genotype The hereditary predisposition of humans, animals or plants. (Psychology) Innate psychological disposition.

Gustatory spectrum Taste.

Habenula, lateral Decision area. A brain nucleus that is one of the smallest regions of our brain. The lateral habenula is most likely responsible for judgment and is essential to our ability to make decisions. When the lateral habenula is disabled, one will be indifferent to choices.

Heuristic A way to make decisions when no logical solution presents itself. The vast majority of decisions and positions that we take on all kinds of issues, are based on the use of heuristic emotions. Formed from the Greek heuriskein (to discover); 1. The doctrine of finding, the science of using a methodical way to discover or invent; 2. Method to solve problems, discover; people often use sloppy thinking rules or heuristics.

Heuristics Provides individuals with the opportunity to find rules and truths by themselves.

Hippocampus Also called the archicortex. The hippocampus (Greek for sea horse) is found in both brain hemispheres. The hippocampus manages episodic memory and short-term memory (working memory). Observations and thoughts that recently required attention are temporarily stored in the hippocampus.

Hue Colour: red, blue, green, yellow, black, white, etc.

Hypophysis The pituitary gland. Located in the middle of the head, beneath the brain. The hypophysis secretes and plays a major role in the regulation of a large number of hormones. It is attached to the hypothalamus through a portal vein system. The hypophysis and the hypothalamus continually monitor hormone levels in the blood to see whether more or less of a particular hormone is required.

Hypothalamus See also thalamus (Hypo-). A small organ managing essential bodily functions, such as changes in heart rate, respiration, body temperature, and hydration (sweat). It also controls sexual behaviour. Along with the hypophysis, the hypothalamus is a part of the diencephalon, below the thalamus.

Inhibition Behavioural inhibition is situated in the prefrontal cortex. Inhibition is essential to a variety of things, from cognitive filtering of less relevant data or observations to controlling emotions. The prefrontal cortex is closely linked to the amygdala, which stores (mostly negative) emotions. Think of the grief caused by the loss of a loved one. See also: Ventromedial Prefrontal Cortex (vmPFC).

Insula / insular cortex The insula or 'the island of Reil' is a part of the brain on the lateral surfaces of the large cerebral hemispheres. The brain area is named after the German anatomist Johann Christian Reil. The functions of the insula are complex and varied. It is assumed that the area processes sensory stimuli into a coherent emotion.

Introspection Self-observation, self-evaluation, explicit memory; conscious memories.

Kinesthetic From the Greek kinèsis (motion) + aisthèsis (feeling). The ability to be aware of the direction and scope of movement; usefulness of movement.

Lateral On the outside or flank; opposite of medial: on the inside.

Libido Psychic energy of sexual desire; the urge to live (reproduction).

Linguistic brain Area of the brain where the language center is situated.

Mammillary body Responsible for spatial memory. The mammillary body is a switch for signals from the hippocampus and the amygdala to the thalamus, a system called the Papez circuit.

Memory, episodic, contextual, working, explicit, primary, declarative Short-term memory. Memory accessible by the mind, often connected to time, place, or factual knowledge. Short-term memory also functions as working memory, which is used, for example, when mentally calculating, in case some results need to be remembered to calculate the final result.

Memory, implicit Unconscious memory, experience.

Memory, semantic Long-term memory. Long-term potentiation (LTP). Potentiation = strengthen, make more powerful.

Morphology Study of the shape and build of organisms. Syn. theory of forms.

MTCA Male Testosterone Causing Aggression.

Neurological development process:

A) Development The developmental process in the embryonic stage, which takes place approximately 7 weeks after conception, influenced (male) or not (female) by testosterone. Determines the male or female characteristics of the physical sex.

B) Transformation The developmental process in the embryonic stage in which the cell structure changes into a male or female form, regulating sexual behaviour.

C) Formation of typical male or female gender-roles The hormonal process taking place during adolescence, along with behaviour, completes and strengthens things such as aggression, social behaviour, individualism, sense of adventure, and shyness.

Neurons (brain cells) Our brain contains 40 billion neurons. Also called ganglion cells.

Noradrenaline (or norepinephrine) A hormone produced in the adrenal cortex, with effects similar to adrenaline. People with too little noradrenaline generally feel depressed, and people with too much noradrenaline feel euphoric, tense, anxious, or excited.

Nucleus accumbens It literally means 'adjacent core'. Enjoyment center or limbic association center. This core group is classified as one of the basal ganglia and is called the ventral striatum. The nucleus accumbens is believed to play an important role in positive experiences, such as desire, motivation, passion, and satisfaction. This brain area also plays a role in love. The nuclei respond to the rewarding effects of behaviour. They presumably not only play a role in addictive behaviour, but also in sexuality, games, and emotions generated by listening to music. In general, the nucleus accumbens has greater involvement in pleasurable short-term activities.

Olfactory system See Smell.

Oxytocin The hormone stimulating the feeling of connectedness. It is released when, for example, long-term partners embrace each other or their children, or when a mother breastfeeds her child. This hormone also strengthens monogamous behaviour.

Physiology Branch of biology dealing with the functions and activities of living organisms and their parts, including all physical and chemical processes.

Physiotherapy Movement therapy; study of movement.

Pineal gland The epiphysis cerebri, or pineal gland, reacts to light and plays various roles in human functioning. Pineal gland hormones regulate a series of biological processes, which are related to the awake and sleeping state. The pineal gland produces the hormones; serotonin, melatonin, and dimethyltryptamine (DMT). DMT is related to the neurotransmitter serotonin.

PMS Premenstrual stress.

Pons The pons, also called the 'bridge of Varolius', is the connection between the cerebellum and cerebrum. The pons ensures that stimuli from the cerebrum, such as from the vestibular system and hearing organs, are transferred to the cerebellum. The front part of the pons is important when sending sensory information, mainly about movement, to the cerebrum. The rear portion of the pons assists in breathing, taste, and sleep.

Primates An order that includes prosimians, monkeys, apes, and humans.

Progesterone Hormone belonging to the class of steroids produced by the corpus luteum or the placenta, which prepares the uterine lining for implantation of a fertilized ovum.

Promiscuity State of society of completely free sexual relations between men and women.

Protos Greek for first, indicating the colour red.

Puberty 13-year-old boy, 12-year-old girl.

Representations Depiction, display, performance, presentation, act in place. The mental images of the world, of objects (a car) and events (a carnival). How brands are represented in our memory. Representations can be divided into three different forms:

1. Analog: Direct storage of visual, auditory, tactile, and smell sensations.

2. Verbal: Verbal representations are linguistic.

3. Propositional: Pertains to the meaning of things. Abstract meanings, non-verbal, and non-visual. Propositions are language-independent. An image.

Retina When we look at a chair, for example, its image is projected onto the retina. This image is then translated into nerve impulses by the retina receptors, which are sent to the thalamus through the nerve fibers of the visual cortex. The thalamus sends these signals to the visual cortex (cerebral cortex), where the image is compared with the image of a chair that has been stored by long-term potentiation (LTP). If the images are sufficiently similar, the chair will be recognized as such.

Rods Responsible for sight in low light conditions. We do not see colour with the rods, only black and white, black and white. Rods are used in peripheral vision (within 180 degrees). The eye contains approximately 123 million rods. Achromatic subsystem for the perception of brightness. The rods provide 5x better visual acuity and enable faster observation.

Sensibility Sensitivity. 1. The ability to perceive pain, pressure, and proprioception (perception of your own body posture). 2. Strongly respond to minor stimuli (easily influenced emotionally).

Septum The septum pellicidum (in short: septum) is a thin triangular vertical membrane that forms the separation between the lateral ventricles in the brain. The septum is involved in the regulation of emotions. There are many links between the septum and the amygdala, the hippocampus, the hypothalamus, and the cortex cerebri (large cerebral cortex). This suggests that the septum serves as a type of connection point between the cognitive processes (cortex and hippocampus) and the emotional processes (amygdala and hypothalamus).

Serotonin One of the main neurotransmitters associated with mood, self-confidence, sleep, emotion, sexual activity, and appetite. People in love (and people with obsessive-compulsive disorder [OCD]) exhibit serotonin levels approximately 40% lower than in people who are not in love. Researchers suspect that people who might be suffering from OCD have a serotonin imbalance. It also plays a role in the processing of pain stimuli. Serotonin has an excitatory effect and works as a regulator of the dopamine system. The serotonergic neurons release serotonin into the brain, which runs to various parts, including the prefrontal cortex. This area plays a major role in, for example, addiction and aggression.

Smell Also called the olfactory system or stimulus. Smell is abstract and is hard to describe. Smell, unlike other senses (sight, hearing, taste, and touch), is directly connected to the limbic system, particularly the amygdala and hippocampus. Smells evoke episodic connections from the episodic memory (hippocampus: short-term memory). The limbic system is very sensitive to analog communication, such as smell. All the information that comes in through our various senses passes through the amygdala. It is believed that the amygdala also stores emotions (and senses associated with emotions, such as smell). Although smells are not primarily being stored, they are involved in the emotional coloration of memory (Franzen & Bouwman, 1999). Smells are suggestive, stimulate associations, and evoke emotions (Schaffelaars 1999).

Soma See Cell body.

Stimulus A sensory response that finds its way to specialized parts of the brain through the thalamus, such as the visual, auditory, and gustatory cortex. See also Cues.

Stress A condition that is often the result of thoughts. Negative thought processes cost energy and cause hormones such as adrenaline and noradrenaline to be released. These hormones increase alertness and prepare the body for fight or flight. The stress hormone cortisol is then released to bring the body back to a status quo.

Substantia nigra The substantia nigra (Latin for black substance) is one of the basal ganglia of the central nervous system. The substantia nigra plays a major role in movement, learning, and addiction.

Tactile sensitivity The touch stimulus consists of 4 primary elements: pressure, pain, heat, and cold. Tickling, for example, is a combination of pain and pressure. Women are extremely sensitive to pressure exerted on the skin, on almost every part of the body. This tactile sensitivity in both young and adult females is significantly higher than in men, to the extent that the results of some trials on women did not even overlap the male results. It was proven that the least sensitive woman had a better sense of touch the most sensitive man (Moir & Jessel, 1990).

Taxon Scientific classification. Biological name for categories, such as variety, kind, gender, family, and so on.

Taxonomy Classification, teaching, and study of biological classifications and systematics.

Testosterone Male sex hormone. Causes an increase in aggressiveness, desire to compete, assertiveness, self-confidence, and independence. Spurs concentration, purpose, motivation, and ambition.

Tetrachromats Women who can perceive 4 colour channels instead of 3. They are sensitive to a colour between red and green. It is theoretically possible that a woman inherits a X chromosome with 2 slightly different red (or green) pigments, while the other X chromosome carries normal pigment genes. Add the biological phenomenon of the X-inactivation, which ensures that some cells focus on the one X-chromosome and other cells on the other. A possible consequence is a woman whose eyes contain 4 different types of cones: blue, green, red, and a slightly different red.

Thalamus Gateway for all sensory information such as sight, hearing, taste, and touch (excluding olfactory senses). The thalamus (sensory relay) is fused to the hypothalamus on the bottom. It is an important switching station for all kinds of information from the senses on its way to the cerebral cortex, but it is also part of the brain circuits that are involved in the control of movement and emotions.

Hypothalamus The hypothalamus regulates blood pressure, heart rate, hunger, thirst, sleep-wake rhythm, sexual arousal, and body temperature (for example, ensures shivering when cold). The hypothalamus is largely responsible for homeostasis and plays a role in three core behaviours: fight or flight response, eating behaviour and reproductive behaviour.

Subthalamus Also called the subthalamic nucleus. A group of neurons beneath the thalamus, which might be involved with regulating posture. The subthalamus is sometimes considered one of the basal ganglia.

Trichromats Humans that perceive colours normally.

Trichromats, anomalous Anomalous means abnormal; cases in which something is wrong with the perception of one of the colours.

Tritos Greek for third, indicating the colour blue.

Ventral Ventral: stomach side; opposite of dorsal: back side.

Ventral Tegmental Area (VTA) A collection of neurons in the center of the brainstem. This section provides basic sensory stimuli to other parts of the brain, ensuring the core functions run smoothly. It is also the area where many pleasant feelings are born and it plays a major role in leisure, drug addiction, and mental illness.

Ventromedial prefrontal cortex (vmPFC) Plays a major role in the inhibition of the amygdala and in the decision-making process. See also Inhibition.

Visual stimulus Observe, watch.

Wavelengths Red 500–700, Green 500–600, Blue 400–500. Cones can be divided into 3 types of cells: short, middle, and long wavelength cells (Young Hermholtz theory). Every group of cones splits the light into their particular wavelength: red, green, or blue.

Literature and relevant chapters

- Bergsma, A., Petersen, & K. Het brein van A tot Z (2nd ed.). The Hague: Hersenstichting The Netherlands, 2003.
- Brizendine, L., Campenhout, & L. De vrouwelijke hersenen: Waarom vrouwen anders zijn dan mannen. Amsterdam, The Netherlands: Sirene, 2007.
- Dabbs, J.M., & Dabbs, M.G. Heroes, Rogues, and Lovers: Testosterone and Behavior. U.S.: McGraw-Hill Inc., 2001.
- Dudlink, Ad and Clifford, Pamela; The Brain Pack, Singram Company, Ltd., St. Helier, Jersey, Channel Island, 1996.
- Effects of Visual attention, 1997.
- Falck, M., Schaffelaars, D., & Zijlstra, S. Geur & ontwerp. Eindhoven, The Netherlands: Z)OO,1999.
- Fisher, H. E. The first sex: The natural talents of women and how they are changing the world. New York: Random House, 1999.
- Floor, J. M., & Raaij, W. F. Marketingcommunicatiestrategie: Reclame, online marketingcommunicatie, public relations en voorlichting, sponsoring, promoties, directmarketingcommunicatie, winkelcommunicatie, persoonlijke verkoop, evenementen, geïntegreerde communicatie (6th ed.). Groningen, The Netherlands: Noordhoff, 2010.
- Franzen, Giep & Bouwman, Margot; De mentale wereld van merken, 1999.
- Franzen, Giep; Wat drijft ons?, denken over motivatie sinds Darwin. Utrecht, The Netherlands: LEMMA, 2004.
- Gerritsen, M., Verdonk, T. & Visser, A. Monitor Vrouwelijke Hoogleraren, 2012.
- Gray, John, Mannen komen van Mars, Vrouwen van Venus; Het Spectrum B.V., Utrecht, The Netherlands, 284 pages, 2003.
- Gregory, Richard L.; Eye and brain, de psychology of seeing, 1997.
- Haan, de; Visuele waarneming, de psychologie van het zien, De Haan, 1970.
- Hofstede, G. Allemaal andersdenkenden: Omgaan met cultuurverschillen (17th ed.). Amsterdam, The Netherlands etc.: Olympus, 2004.
- Kotler, P., Broere, F., Armstrong, G., Saunders, J., & Wong, V. Principes van marketing (5th ed.). Amsterdam, The Netherlands: Pearson Education, 2009.
- Kuypers, Klaartje; De effecten van herhaling, Blad/dossier, (8th ed.) from a series of 8, Effect & accountability, 1994.
- Lamme, V. A. De vrije wil bestaat niet: Over wie er echt de baas is in het brein (12th ed.). Amsterdam, The Netherlands: Bakker, 2011. Amsterdam: Stichting de Beauvoir.
- Masculinity & Feminity, An Empirical Definition, 1991.
- Moir, Anne en Jessel, David; Het grote verschil tussen man en vrouw, waarom hersenstructuur mannen en vrouwen zo verschillend maakt, 1990.
- Moir, A., Jessel, D. Brain Sex: The Real Difference Between Men and Women New York: Dell, 1991.
- Noord, Henk; Vrouwen willen maar één ding...; The house of books, Vianen/Antwerpen, 205 pages, 2005.
- Piontek, M. D., Koekoek, M., & Palitzsch-Schulz, A. Het wonder van de vrouwelijke seksualiteit: Werkboek voor vrouwen. Haarlem, The Netherlands: Altamira, 2012.
- Plessis, E. D., & Walsmit, V. Reclame en ons brein. Alphen aan den Rijn, The Netherlands: Samsom, 2001.
- Psychology en sekse, 1992.
- Putten, Katja van; Fé.losofie/Fé.nominaal, 2003. Rode, H. A., Mertz, P., & Blank, F. Ontwikkelingen en trends in organisatie en bedrijf. Deventer, The Netherlands: Kluwer, 1987.
- Scherder, E. Laat je hersenen niet zitten: Hoe lichaamsbeweging de hersenen jong houdt (2nd ed.). Amsterdam, The Netherlands: Athenaeum Polak & Van Gennep, 2014.
- Sterling, A.F. Sexing the Body: Gender Politics and the Construction of Sexuality. New York, NY: Basic, 2000 Books.
- Swaab, D. F., & Kunen, M. Wij zijn ons brein: Van baarmoeder tot Alzheimer (41st ed.). Amsterdam, The Netherlands: Olympus, 2015.
- Underhill, Paco; Waarom we kopen wat we kopen, De wetenschap ven het winkelen (Original title: Why We Buy), The science of shopping); 2000-Forum-Amsterdam, 267 pages, 1999.
- Vroon, Piet; Amerongen, Anton van en Vries, Hans de; Verborgen verleider, Psychologie van de reuk, AMBO/Baarn, 217 pages, 1994.
- Vroon, Piet; Tranen van de krokodil. Amsterdam: Ambo/Anthos Uitgevers, 2006.

Articles from: the internet, opinion magazines, trade journals, university libraries and articles in scientific journals.

- Alexander, R.S.; Some Aspects of Sex Differences in Relation to Marketing, Journal of Marketing; 12, 000002; ABI/INFORM Global, pp., 158-171, 1986 (October 1947).
- Assessibility: Effectief omgaan met kleuren, 21 pages, 2003.
- Bartos R.; Advertising to Women, World Advertising Research Centre, WARC Advice, Admap, September 1995.
- Boomsma, Diana & Paoletti, Jim; A review of current research on the effects of Progesterone, International Journal of Pharmaceutical Compounding, Vol. 6, No. 4, July/August 2002.
- Brettel, Hans; Vienot, Francoise en Mollon, John; Vischchek, Journal of the Optical Society of America, Vol. 14, No. 10 pp. 2647, 2004.
- Brunt, Emma; De piekerziekte, HP/DE TIJD pp. 68 - 69; 21 January 2005.
- Cahill, Larry; his brain, her brain (differences in male and female brains), Scientific American, pp. 22-29, Vol. 292, No. 5, May 2005.
- Camps, Hugo; Bij mannen zie je vaak dat jongetje, interview met Cisca Dresselhuys, beroepsfeministe, Elsevier: pp. 36 - 38, 24 February, 2001.
- Clercq, Wouter de; Stereotypes in reclame: impliciete attitudes ten opzichte van de nieuwe man, Scriptie: 85 pages, Universiteit Gent, TheNetherlands, Faculteit Economie en Bedrijfskunde, Thesisyear 2002-2003.
- Conner, Psy.D., Michael G., Clinical & medical Psychologist, Oregon Counseling, Understanding The Difference Between Men And Woman, copyright: Michael G. Conner, 1999-2000.
- Coumans, Anke; Visuele Communicatie of Hoe wij beelden interpreteren, 35 pages; Hogeschool voor de Kunsten Utrecht, The Netherlands; Faculteit Beeldende Kunst en Vormgeving; afdeling Visuele Communicatie, 2000.
- Davidson, Michael W. and Abramowitz, Mortimer; Human vision and colour perception; Olympus America Inc., and The Florida State University, 1 August, 1998.
- Evers, Catharine; Sekseverschillen in boosheid; UvA, Faculteit der maatschappij en gedragswetenschappen, Psychologie: Sociale Psychologie, 2004.
- Frankplads, P.C. 'The Human Sexes' by Desmond Morris - episode 1: Different But Equal (FULL) [Video file]. Received from http://www.youtube.com/watch?v=cvsmD5OqO0w, 2013, 4 July.
- Gur, R.C., Alsop, D., Glahn, D., Petty, R., Swanson, C.L., Maldjian, ... , & Gur, R.E. An fMRI Study of Sex Differences in Regional Activation to a Verbal and a Spatial Task. Brain and Language, 74, pp. 157 - 170, 2000.
- Hansen, Kurt; Verschillend maar gelijk, de visie van Desmond Morris op de verschillen tussen mannen en vrouwen, internet, RKG. 12 May, 2002.
- Hansen. Received from: http://www.rkg.be/rkg5/page32/page43/page43.html
- Heijnen, Halmar; Vrouwen kopen 80% van alles wat verkocht wordt; Nieuwsbrief Wegener huis-aan-huiskranten, Vol. 8, No. 3, September 2005; Mediaweek June 2005, huis-aan-huiskranten bereiksonderzoek June, 2004.
- Hupfer, Maureen; Communicating with the Agentic Woman and the Communal Man: Are Stereotypic Advertising Appeals Stil Relevant? Mc Master University, Academy of Marketing Science Review, No. 3, 17 pages, Vol. 2002.
- Jongh, Reinoud de; Populaire misverstanden (het verdeelde brein), Psychologie Magazine, pp. 36 - 38, 24e year, July/August 2005.
- Kalloniatis, Michael and Luu, Charles; The Perception of Colour, John Moran Eye Center University of Utah, 2000.
- Kamsma, Martine; Vrouw is gewoon slimmer, maar carrière is mannending; Het Parool, The Netherlands, category science, May, 2003.
- Khouw, Natalia; The Meaning of Colour for Gender, 5 pages, Colour Matters- Research, 1998.
- Kimura, Doreen; Human sex differences in cognition: fact, not predicament, Sexualities, Evolution & Gender, 6, pp. 45 - 53, Simon Fraser University, BC, Canada, 2004.
- Kimura, Doreen; Sex Differences in the Brain, 10 pages; Scientific American September, 1992.
- Kimura, Doreen; Sex Hormones Influence Human Cognitive Pattern, PH.D.,F.R.S.C., L.L.D. (Hon.), Neuroendocrinology Letters Special Issue; 23 (suppl. 4): pp. 67-77, 2002.
- Kimura, Doreen and Clarke, Paul; Women's advantage on verbal memory is not restricted to concrete words, Psychological Reports, 2002, 91, pp. 1137 - 1142, 2002.
- Wikipedia. Young–Helmholtz theory - Wikipedia, the free encyclopedia. Retrieved from https://en.wikipedia.org/wiki/Young–Helmholtz_theory 25 October, 2015.
- Koolen, G. Managers: vrouw versus man, een vergelijking in 7 landen, 2014, Received from http://www.lugerarepublic.nl/lugeranlFiles/home-flayers/2014/april/Vrouw%20versus%20man,%20een%20vergelijking%20in%207%20landenpdf.

- KUN, Nijmegen Neuroscience Nieuwsbrief: Into the brain, 2003.
- Leclaire, A., & Zandstra, F. Jong, vrouw & ziek. HP De Tijd, July, 2000.
- List, dr. G.A. van der; RUG: Marsmannetjes en venusvrouwtjes, over de maatschappelijke betekenis van sekseverschillen, Liberaal Reveil, pp. 99 - 104, 1999.
- Lokhorst, Gert-Jan. C.; Intermediair, Nobelprijs geneeskundefysiologie 1981: Roger W. Sperry., 17 (50): 7-9, ISSN 0020-5605, December 11, 1981.
- MacLean, P. D., & Kral, V. A. A triune concept of the brain and behaviour. Published for the Ontario Mental Health Foundation by University of Toronto Press, 1973.
- Malfroot, A., Brugada, P., Maselis, T., Van Damme, P., & Van Middelem, G. Erfelijke aandoeningen, 2013, Received from http://www.gezonheid.be/index. cfm?fuseaction=art&art_id=2946
- McEwen, B.S. Steroid Hormones: Effect on Brain Development and Function. Hormone, 1992, Research in Paediatrics, 37(3), 1-10. DOI:10.1159/000182393
- Meyers-Levy, Joan and Sternthal, Brain JMR; Gender Differences in the Use of Message Cues and Judgement, Journal of Marketing Research; 28, 1; ABI/INFORM Global; pp. 84 - 96, February, 1991.
- Meyers-Levy, Joan; The influence of Sex Roles on Judgment, Journal of Consumer Research, pp. 522 - 530, Vol. 14, ABI/INFORM Global, March, 1988.
- Mieras, Mark; Binnenkijken in het brein, Psychologie magazine. pp. 38 - 43, May, 2005.
- Moutinho, Luiz and Goode, Mark; Gender Effects to the Formation of Overall Product Satisfaction: A multivariate Approach; Journal of International Consumer Marketing; 8, 1; ABI/INFORM Global; pp. 71 - 91, 1995.
- Murphy, P. Chaos Theory as a model for Managing Issues and Crises. Public Relations Review, 22(2), pp. 95 - 113, 1996.
- Oudakker, Gwen; Cebuco Nieuws, Wat vinden lezers van de advertentie?, Vol. 7, No. 27, September, 2005.
- Parool, Het; Sekseverschillen in gebruik internet, July 2000.
- Pieters, Rik; Een beetje Invite en heel veel Marieke, Aandacht voor reclame steeds moeilijker te vangen; Tijdschrift voor de Marketing, No. 3, Vol. 32, pp. 20 - 23, March, 1998.
- Pieters, Rik; Oog voor reclame, Eye-tracking wordt betrouwbaar en betaalbaar; Tijdschrift voor de Marketing, Vol. 32, No. 4, pp. 16 - 19, April, 1998.
- Putrevu Sanjay; Exploring the Origins and Information Processing Differences Between Men and Women: Implications for Advertisers; Academy of Marketing Science Review; 2001, ABI/INFORM Global; 16 pages, 2001.
- Raaij, Prof dr. W.F.; Van consumentengedrag, een bijdrage vanuit de economische psychologie, 2000.
- Reinisch, J.M., Sanders, S.A. Prenatal Gonadal Steroidal Influences on Gender-Related Behavior. Progress in Brain Research, 61, pp. 407 - 416, 1984.
- Richel, Theo; Het agressieve geslacht; HP/DE TIJD, pp. 22 - 30, 20 June, 2003.
- Rozendaal, Simon; 33 verschillen tussen haar & hem, Elsevier: pp. 66 - 72, 20 July, 2002.
- Sabbatini, PhD, Renato M.E.; Magazine: Brain & Mind, Are There Differences between the Brains of Males and Females, 4 pages, copyright: State University of Campinas, 1997.
- Sandin, Ev-Lina en Äkäslompolo, Nadja; (Thesis) Business Administration and Social Sciences; Developing Advertising Messages, Luleå University of Technology; 67 pages, June 2004.
- Severson, A. Testosterone Levels by Age, 2013, Received from http://www.healthline.com/health/low-testosterone/testosterone-levels-by-age
- Sheeve, James; De geest is wat het brein doet. Hoe werkt het brein, National Geographic: pp. 2 - 21 March, 2005.
- Thinkquest: Sekseverschillen in het brein, 3 pages; Evolutie, 2 pages; Emoties, 2 pages; Stress, 2 pages; Angst, 2 pages; Het lange termijn geheugen, 2 pages; Het korte termijn geheugen, 1 pages; Zintuigen, 3 pages; De lay-out van de hersenen, 3 pages; Zenuwcellen, 2 pages; Gebieden, 2 pages; Hersenhelften, 2 pages, 2002.
- Tobias, Sheila; 'Niet dom, maar anders', UT- nieuws, Vol. 31, nr. 35, Weekblad van de Universiteit Twente, 3 pages, 21 November 1996.
- Traa, Mark; Hormonen onder de waterspiegel, HP DE TIJD, pag. 12 - 13, 11 March 2005.
- Universiteit Twente The Netherlands, UT nieuws, Taalgebruik en de gevolgen ervan.
- UvT bibliotheek; Gender differences in human cognition, De eeuwige zoektocht naar sekseverschillen, 1997.
- Vaal, D. de; Zien tetrachromaten wat wij niet zien? Science, 2 pages, 30 November, 2000.
- Vries, G.J. de; Sex differences in neurotransmitters in the brain, PubMed, National Library of Medicine, 1990.
- Waguespack, N.M. The Organization of Male and Female Labor in Foraging Societies: Implications for Early Paleoindian Archaeology. American Anthropologist, 107(4), 666-676, 2005.

- Wiering, Connie; Marketing is geen vrouwenberoep. Sekse en beloning, ambitie, functioneren. Cover: Tijdschrift voor de marketing, pp. 12 - 18, (9th ed.), Vol. 39, September 2005.
- Wikipedia, De vrije encyclopedie; nl.wikipedia.org, opgezochte woorden: Amygdala, Hippocampus, Thalamus, Hypothalamus, Kleine hersenen, Zintuigen en Basale Ganglia, 8 pages, July 2005.
- Wytzes, Liesbeth; Vrouw en nokkenas. Vrouwen kopen steeds meer auto's, maar het jargon schrikt ze nog af. Een website bied hulp; rubriek: Auto, Elsevier 12 March, 2005.

Qualitative research (interview)

G. Key, personal communication, 2005.

M. de Jong, personal communication, 2005.

P. Wolff, personal communication, 2005.

D. Sille, personal communication, 2005.

L.W.H.L. Hulsebos, personal communication, 2005.

E. Capello, personal communication, 2005.

P. van Nunen, personal communication, 2005.

Images (Shutterstock)

- Zajac, P. (2013, May 18). *Harley Davidson motorbikes parade* [Photograph]. Retrieved from www.shutterstock.com, picture number 138953810
- Firenze, B. (2014, March 20). virtual reality headset [photograph]. Retrieved from www.shutterstock.com, picture number 190604936

Advertisements

- Abbott Mead Vickers (AMV) BBDO, London. (n.d.). The Economist [Advertisement]. Retrieved from www.plus.google.com/photos, The Economist
- Abbott Mead Vickers (AMV) BBDO, London. (n.d.). Whiskas [Advertisement]. Retrieved from www.luerzersarchive.com
- Bartle Bogle Hegarty (BBH), London. (1996). FABERGÉ [Advertisement]. Retrieved from www.luerzersarchive.com
- BBDO, Brazil. (2013). Pedigree [Advertisement]. Retrieved from www.adsoftheworld.com
- Blahblahism, Amsterdam. (2013). Capi Europe [Guerilla campaign]. Retrieved from www.blahblahism.com
- Carmichael Lynch, Minneapolis. (n.d.). Porsche [Advertisement]. Retrieved from www.luerzersarchive.com
- Cloeck & Moedigh film en projectiereclame, Amsterdam, The Netherlands. (1950). DAF [Advertisement]. Retrieved from www.gehegenvannederland nl
- DDB & Tribal, Amsterdam. (2010). Mac Donalds [TV Commercial]. Retrieved from www.youtube.com, McDonalds Mannenburgers 'passen'
- DDB, Barcelona. (n.d.). Chupa Chups [Advertisement]. Retrieved from www.luerzersarchive.com
- DDB, Brussels. (n.d.). Audi [Advertisement]. Retrieved from www.luerzersarchive.com
- Début Art, London. (n.d.). Coca-Cola Raspberry [Advertisement]. Retrieved from www.debutart.com
- DM9DDB, Sao Paulo. (1999). Parmalat [Advertisement]. Retrieved from www.advertolog.com
- DM9DDB, São Paulo. (n.d.). Valisère [Advertisement]. Retrieved from www.luerzersarchive.com
- DMB&B Worldwide communications, Netherlands. (n.d.). Bavaria [Advertisement]. Retrieved from Art Directors Club Nederland, Annual 1995
- Grey, Canada. (2013). Moms Demand Action [Advertisement]. Retrieved from www.adsoftheworld.com
- Inhalt & Form, Switzerland. (2013). Black & Blaze [Advertisement]. Retrieved from www.adsoftheworld.com
- Jung von Matt, Hamburg. (1998). BMW [Advertisement]. Retrieved from www.luerzersarchive.com
- J. Walter Thomson (JWT), London. (n.d.). Diamond Information Centre [Advertisement]. Retrieved from World advertising review, 1998
- KKBR/SMS, Amsterdam. (n.d.). Minolta [Advertisement]. Retrieved from Art Director Annual Nederland, 1991
- Leo Burnett, London. (n.d.). John West [Advertisement]. Retrieved from www.luerzersarchive.com
- Leo Burnett, London. (n.d.). Mercedes-Benz [Advertisement]. Retrieved from www.luerzersarchive.com
- Levallois Perret, Australia . (n.d.). Contrex [Advertisement]. Retrieved from www.luerzersarchive.com
- L'Oréal, Paris. [Advertisement]. Retrieved from http://hdimagelib.com/cosmetics+brands?image=391059303
- M&C Saatchi, Sydney. (n.d.). Beverly Hills [Advertisement]. Retrieved from www.luerzersarchive.com
- M&C Saatchi, Sydney. (n.d.). Beverly Hills [Advertisement]. Retrieved from www.luerzersarchive.com

- Proximity, Bangkok. (2013). BMW [Advertisement]. Retrieved from www.coloribus.com
- Publicis, Amsterdam. (n.d.). Nestle The Netherlands, MAGGI [Advertisement]. Retrieved from Allerhande, Albert Heijn The Netherlands
- Revolution Brasil, Brazil. (2013). Star Models [Advertisement]. Retrieved from www.advertolog.com
- Robijn, Netherlands. (2014). Unilever, Robijn [Advertisement]. Retrieved from www.facebook.com/robijndoetdewas/photos
- Saatchi & Saatchi, Dubai. (2008). Olay, P&G [Advertisement]. Retrieved from www.advertolog.com
- Saatchi & Saatchi, Lyon. (2015). Toyota [Advertisement]. Retrieved from www.behance.net
- Springer & Jacoby, Germany. (2004). Harley Davidson [Advertisement]. Retrieved from www.coloribus.com
- Strating Promotion, Amsterdam, The Netherlands. (n.d.). Amstel [Advertisement]. Retrieved from www.luerzersarchive.com
- TBWA\Hunt\Lascaris, Johannesburg. (n.d.). BIC [Advertisement]. Retrieved from www.luerzersarchive.com
- TBWA\Neboko, Amsterdam The Netherlands. (2002). Delta Lloyd [Advertisement]. Retrieved from www.advertolog.com
- Tonic International, Dubai. (2011). Audi [Advertisement]. Retrieved from www.adsoftheworld.com
- Ubachs Wisbrun, Amsterdam. (n.d.). MG Nederland [Advertisement]. Retrieved from Annual 2000, Art Directors Club The Netherlands
- vOSCH The Brand Guide, Netherlands. (2009). Droste [Advertisement]. Retrieved from www.vosch.nl
- vOSCH The Brand Guide, Netherlands (2004). Floris van Bommel [Advertisement]. Retrieved from www.vosch.nl
- Weigert Pirouz Wolf Werbeagentur GmbH., Hamburg. (n.d.). Schuhe Blicker [Advertisement]. Retrieved from www.luerzersarchive.com
- Young & Rubicam (Y&R), Madrid. (n.d.). Ford [Advertisement]. Retrieved from www.luerzersarchive.com